Where has this book been? Now that we have it, what did the church ever do without it, and can I ever not have it nearby? I am savoring this book like a black iron skillet that gets better with age and will use it to cook up some theological dishes I never thought possible.

LEONARD SWEET
Author of *From Tablet to Table* and creator of preachthestory.com

We lose time, save time, waste time, find time. But what about inhabiting time? That is Michelle Van Loon's important invitation through her well-studied exploration of the Jewish and Christian calendars. She bids us to keep holy days (not just holidays) and relieve our cultural anxiety that time is running out.

JEN POLLOCK MICHEL
Author of *Teach Us to Want*

One of God's earliest gifts to Israel after forming them into a covenant people was a calendar to celebrate and to remind Israel of the major moments of God's redemption. Israel's year was shaped by those redemptive events so that every major holiday was simultaneously a memorial of God's gracious redemption. The New Testament era of history was not long enough to form a Christian calendar, and even more the Jewish Christians already had their own calendar—which they were adapting and adjusting in their worship of the Messiah. So it was nothing but Spirit-led wisdom for the church as it spread into the Roman Empire to adapt the Jewish calendar into a Christian calendar. Michelle Van Loon's wise, readable, and informed study of the two calendars is a gift for all of us. Try one year of using the Christian calendar and you will be reminded, not of our presidents or our heroes, but of God's redemption in Christ.

SCOT McKNIGHT
Julius R. Mantey Chair of New Testament, Northern Seminary, and author of *The Jesus Creed*

This wonderful book is full of both information and inspiration about times we call holidays. The author offers rich background on the origins of both Jewish and Christian observances and includes practical ideas for making these times more meaningful. This book will be an invaluable resource for every home and will make a wonderful gift.

DALE HANSON BOURKE
Author of *Everyday Miracles*

This is an absolutely wonderful book for any who want to understand the grace-filled rhythms that God has built in to our days. As a pastor and parent, I cannot recommend this book highly enough!

REVEREND TRACEY BIANCHI
Worship and teaching pastor, Christ Church of Oak Brook, traceybianchi.com

Many books have been written about how to honor God with our talents and treasures but very few about how to honor Him with our time. Michelle has provided a much-needed resource for those who want to benefit from engaging in the sacred festivals within the Jewish calendar that were observed by Jesus himself or the Christian ones that were inspired by his life and ministry. This book will teach you how to see time from God's perspective and how to leverage it for His glory and your delight. A must-read for anyone who takes the Bible—and their days—seriously.

JUSTIN KRON
The Kesher Forum

Herein lies a vast storehouse of riches that Michelle Van Loon unlocks for us. In *Moments & Days*, we discover our spiritual roots and the rhythms of our days. Van Loon, a Jewish follower of Jesus, wisely and deftly explores the formative implications of living by the Jewish and Christian festal calendars throughout the year. Jesus himself was spiritually formed by living according to the festal rhythms. If you long to become more like Jesus, then read this book. It is a unique and important work—a gift. Don't miss out.

MARLENA GRAVES
Author of *A Beautiful Disaster*

MICHELLE VAN LOON

MOMENTS & DAYS

How Our Holy Celebrations Shape Our Faith

A NavPress resource published in alliance
with Tyndale House Publishers, Inc.

NAVPRESS⬤®

NavPress is the publishing ministry of The Navigators, an international Christian organization and leader in personal spiritual development. NavPress is committed to helping people grow spiritually and enjoy lives of meaning and hope through personal and group resources that are biblically rooted, culturally relevant, and highly practical.

For more information, visit www.NavPress.com.

Moments & Days: How Our Holy Celebrations Shape Our Faith

Copyright © 2016 by Michelle Van Loon. All rights reserved.

A NavPress resource published in alliance with Tyndale House Publishers, Inc.

NAVPRESS and the NAVPRESS logo are registered trademarks of NavPress, The Navigators, Colorado Springs, CO. *TYNDALE* is a registered trademark of Tyndale House Publishers, Inc. Absence of ® in connection with marks of NavPress or other parties does not indicate an absence of registration of those marks.

Cover and back cover photographs are the properties of their respective copyright holders, and all rights are reserved: Communion tray © ptnphotof/Adobe Stock. Candles © tashka2000/Adobe Stock. Grapes © kyonnta/Adobe Stock. Passover objects © maglara/Adobe Stock. Alarm clock © Pavlo Kucherov/Adobe Stock. Egg © topnat/123RF Stock.

The Team:
Don Pape, Publisher
David Zimmerman, Acquisitions Editor
Ron Kaufmann, Designer

Published in association with The Steve Laube Agency, 24 W. Camelback Rd. A-635, Phoenix, AZ 85013.

All Scripture quotations, unless otherwise indicated, are taken from the Holy Bible, *New International Version,® NIV.®* Copyright © 1973, 1978, 1984, 2011 by Biblica, Inc.® Used by permission. All rights reserved worldwide. Scripture quotations marked ESV are taken from *The Holy Bible*, English Standard Version® (ESV®), copyright © 2001 by Crossway, a publishing ministry of Good News Publishers. Used by permission. All rights reserved. Scripture quotations marked MSG are taken from *THE MESSAGE* by Eugene H. Peterson, copyright © 1993, 1994, 1995, 1996, 2000, 2001, 2002. Used by permission of NavPress Publishing Group. All rights reserved. Scripture quotations marked NLT are taken from the *Holy Bible*, New Living Translation, copyright © 1996, 2004, 2015 by Tyndale House Foundation. Used by permission of Tyndale House Publishers, Inc., Carol Stream, Illinois 60188. All rights reserved.

Some of the anecdotal illustrations in this book are true to life and are included with the permission of the persons involved. All other illustrations are composites of real situations, and any resemblance to people living or dead is purely coincidental.

Library of Congress Cataloging-in-Publication Data

Names: Van Loon, Michelle, author.
Title: Moments and days : how our holy celebrations shape our faith / Michelle Van Loon.
Description: Colorado Springs : NavPress, 2016. | Includes bibliographical references.
Identifiers: LCCN 2016015629| ISBN 9781631464638 | ISBN 9781631464645 (e-pub) | ISBN 9781631464652 (kindle) | ISBN 9781631464669
Subjects: LCSH: Fasts and feasts—Judaism. | Fasts and feasts in the Bible. | Rites and ceremonies in the Bible. | Fasts and feasts. | Church calendar. | Christianity and other religions—Judaism. | Judaism—Relations—Christianity.
Classification: LCC BM690 .V357 2016 | DDC 263—dc23 LC record available at https://lccn.loc.gov/2016015629

Printed in the United States of America

22	21	20	19	18	17	16
7	6	5	4	3	2	1

To my forever family
(Revelation 19:6-9)

CONTENTS

INTRODUCTION

Take My Moments and My Days

FOR 85 PERCENT OF EACH WEEK, modern Jerusalem is a noisy place. Each year, one and a half million camera-wielding pilgrims jostle for space with the city's eight hundred thousand permanent residents. Mix fervent prayer, the chatter of mothers walking their children to the market in strollers, the dialed-to-eleven volume of debate in cafés and at bus stops, car and taxi horns honking, sirens blaring, and feral cats fighting, and you have a mad symphony of sound.

But as Friday afternoon marches toward sundown, these sounds fade, and the city takes on a remarkable stillness. Save for a few cabs and service vehicles, cars disappear from the streets. Businesses close their doors. Voices dial down their volume from eleven to four. A holy hush descends on the city long before the first star appears in the desert sky over the city.

It is *Shabbat*, the Sabbath. The hush holds the city in its embrace until about an hour or so after sunset on Saturday. The volume builds once again in the early evening darkness as Jerusalem returns to its regularly scheduled program—until the following Friday afternoon.

The first time I experienced Sabbath in Jerusalem, I heard within the silence a loving reminder: There was a story the infinite God was telling us about himself within the finite measures of time that he's given to each one of us. It is a story about who he is and who we are called to be. In our plugged-in, 24/7/365 world drumming to an insistent, unvarying beat every single day, we are prone to miss the cadence of eternity. God has built his own rhythms of restoration and celebration into our days and years.

This book is meant to give us ears to hear them.

TAKE MY MOMENTS AND MY DAYS

I grew up in a fairly secular Jewish home in the suburbs of Chicago, so I knew about Shabbat. At least I thought I did.

On Friday nights, just before we ate dinner, my mom would kindle the two candles that welcomed the Sabbath into our home, and we'd pray the traditional Hebrew blessing over the flickering lights. After those moments of ritual, we'd go back to whatever we were doing—watching TV, doing homework or chores. Once in a great while, my family would visit our local temple for Shabbat morning services. But that level of religious observance was the exception, not the rule, in my Middle American, baby boomer childhood.

I came to faith in my Messiah Jesus as a teen, much to my parents' deep chagrin. Christians have a long, ugly history of persecuting Jewish people, and my parents could not understand why I would join a team with a track record like that. The horrible anti-Semitism exemplified by the Crusades, the pogroms, and the Holocaust was a fabric woven of bitter thorns, entirely different from the love and mercy I'd experienced from my Jewish Savior, Jesus.

I married a young man I met in a Bible study. The bonus for me was that he had a Jewish mom, which made him Jewish too. Bill and I began attending a small Messianic Jewish congregation near our home. These gatherings are designed for Jewish seekers and followers of Jesus, as well as Gentile Christians interested in learning more about the Hebrew foundations of their faith. Some of these gatherings use the liturgy and practice of a Jewish synagogue, while others function more like a Jewish-accented nondenominational church. Most of them orient their worship and celebration around the Jewish calendar cycle.

The Shabbat candles, the Passover meals, attendance at the autumn High Holy Day services at our temple—those bits of childhood ritual I'd experienced took on new meaning as we walked through the weekly and yearly cycle of the Jewish calendar with other Jewish believers. As we worshipped with other Jewish believers each week, the colorful but disconnected puzzle pieces of the faith I'd experienced as a child were being fit into a Jesus-shaped framework. They fit perfectly.

Shortly after our first child was born, we moved to an affordable but far-flung suburb. Continuing to attend the Messianic congregation was no longer practical, so we found our way to a nondenominational evangelical congregation similar to the one in which we'd first met. Several relocations over the next decades kept us living in primarily Gentile communities. We were often the only family of Jewish believers in some of the congregations we attended.

Some church people told me that my Jewishness didn't matter now that I believed in Jesus; the church had replaced Israel in God's plan. Other churches treated us as trophies, a sort of living down payment on a Last Days timeline because we as

Jewish people now believed in Jesus. Despite some of the awkward, uninformed, but usually well-meaning words, our family found a home among evangelical Gentile followers of Jesus. Bill attended an evangelical seminary. I began writing plays, skits, articles, and curriculum for publication, to be used by the church. We were active members of the congregations we attended. Yet in our home we committed to pass on to our children a sense of their Jewish identity, as well as a living faith in their Jewish Messiah. We believed their Jewish identity and a living faith in the resurrected Lord were their birthrights—and our responsibility to pass on to them.

On occasion through the years, my husband and I would be invited to teach Sunday school classes about some of the Old Testament foundations of New Testament faith. We led a number of Passover seders for curious small groups. People were always interested in the story of our respective faith journeys, too. But while I continued to carry a sense of the yearly rhythms of time and worship described in Old Testament Scripture, it seemed simpler somehow to keep "our" holidays as a background beat. Attempting to blend in seemed to be the best way to get along with our Gentile brothers and sisters.

But then two things converged to push the sound of those rhythms—two distinctively different beats—to the foreground.

During our first trip to Israel a few years ago, I experienced a Sabbath where most everyone around me was observing it. The stillness of this place shouted at me. I realized my intellectual understanding of what the day was meant to be fell far short of its actual experience in the context of community. Even those in Jerusalem who weren't particularly religious stayed off the streets from Friday at sundown until the first three stars appeared after

Saturday's sunset. They were drawn into the holy hush of Shabbat by the strong level of observance within the city's predominately Jewish populace. The hush carries into the city's Muslim community, for whom Friday is a day of prayer, and it is respected by the minority Christian groups who have maintained a presence in Jerusalem for centuries.

A fellow Jewish believer in Jesus living in Israel told me that this shared, communal participation in the weekly Sabbath and the yearly cycle of biblical and historical holidays had been a very powerful formative experience in her relationship with the Lord. I caught a glimpse of how that could be true in the silence that draped Jerusalem like a prayer shawl as the sun set each Friday.

A second rhythm occasionally matched the first, but it had its own distinctive beat. My husband and I began attending a congregation that followed the church calendar and used formal liturgy in its worship. All of our previous congregations had a cycle of observance that went something like this:

> Thanksgiving
> Christmas
> Good Friday
> Easter
> Mother's Day
> Father's Day
> church picnic

Our new congregation's yearly cycle began with Advent and moved into Christmastide, then Epiphany, Lent, Holy Week, Easter, and Pentecost, before settling into Ordinary Time. Though I'd long known about the basics of the Christian calendar, it was an entirely different experience to worship through it.

Each of these rhythms invited me to live inside its distinctive cadence. Each one accented a different story about the One who created us and is redeeming and transforming us in real time. As I contemplated the rhythms of stillness in a Jerusalem Sabbath and the music of joyous bells ringing during a Resurrection Day church service, my questions became my prayer:

Lord, what story does the Jewish calendar tell me about you? What do you want me to know about you through the Christian calendar? In light of what I learn, Father, how am I to respond? In this plugged-in, always-on age, what do the answers to those questions have to say about how I live every day—and how my family and my congregation choose to worship you?

My prayed questions gently convicted me. Perhaps I had too small a view of the moments and days I was offering to him. I've always loved the words of Frances Havergal's hymn, "Take My Life and Let It Be." The lyrics provide a way for me to express my desire to surrender myself wholeheartedly to God.

Take my life and let it be
Consecrated, Lord, to Thee.
Take my moments and my days;
Let them flow in endless praise.

Perhaps, in my prayer filled with questions, there was something more than my watch, cell phone, and Day-Timer at stake.

DISCIPLESHIP: FOLLOWING THE QUESTIONS

In our always-connected digital world, many of us have become accustomed to the idea that we are the architects of our days. We make our appointments and set our schedules, all the while kvetching that we're just too busy. Our overscheduled lives proclaim to the world and ourselves that, really, we're superindispensible people. We allow a subtle pride to warp our understanding of our roles in God's story: "Look at my crammed date book! If others need or want me this much, I must be pretty important."

And if they don't, then it's not a far leap for some of us to believe that maybe our lives don't matter much.

I'd like to suggest that our watches and Day-Timers and Google calendars are not the measure of our worth. We who belong to Jesus understand (at least in our heads) that we are not our own. Our eternal God has given us this slice of eternity, right here and now, in which to live for and with him.

Following a calendar that tells us our lives are not all about us is a powerful place to learn to inhabit that sacred gift of time. When Paul acknowledged not all followers of Jesus see specific days as holy, he wasn't suggesting that everyone in the church needed to hit the "Delete" button on the discussion (Romans 14:5-10). He was instead encouraging them to give one another lots of grace as they sought how to honor God together in their community. He never discounted the value of the weekly/yearly rhythm of holy days. He simply wanted the Jewish and Gentile followers of Jesus to understand that the finished work of Jesus the Messiah fills full the meaning of these festival days:

> Do not let anyone judge you by what you eat or drink,
> or with regard to a religious festival, a New Moon

celebration or a Sabbath day. These are a shadow of the things that were to come; the reality, however, is found in Christ. COLOSSIANS 2:16-17

That reality must shape our ordinary moments and our sacred days. For those of us who find our spiritual identity determined by our own schedules, growth in discipleship may well mean choosing instead to be formed by the rhythms of appointed times with God in our individual lives and in our church communities. Those holy days are gifts of love from God designed to help us understand the nature of eternal life.

Rabbi Jack Reimer offers a wonderful explanation about the difference between the kinds of holidays that populate our own calendars and the everyday eternity of a holy day:

> *On holidays we run away from duties. On holy days we face up to them. On holidays we let ourselves go. On holy days we try to bring ourselves under control. On holidays we try to empty our minds. On holy days we attempt to replenish our spirits. On holidays we reach out for the things we want. On holy days we reach up for the things we need. Holidays bring a change of scene. Holy days bring a change of heart.*[1]

This book is designed to give you helpful, illuminating information about our rich biblical heritage of holy days, along with practical inspiration as you consider these questions for yourself. Together we'll explore the gift of time and take a brief look at the relationship of the Jewish and Christian calendars and their stories, structures, and histories. You'll find short chapters about each key holy day or season in both calendars that include

> Bible background;
> an explanation of how observance of the holy day has changed through history;
> a look at how Jesus' life and ministry fulfilled (or will fulfill at his return) the heart of each sacred appointment in time; and
> some practical suggestions about how you, your family, and your congregation might step into the day or season.

These holy days aren't a pile-on of additional to-dos for your busy life. They are instead a way for you to create intentionality in the way you live the gift of eternal life God has given you through his Son. My prayer for each of us is that we will have ears to hear the rhythm of eternity as we consider the ways in which we live each moment and day of our lives.

Teach us to number our days,
    that we may gain a heart of wisdom.

PSALM 90:12

1

MEASURING TIME, BEING MEASURED BY TIME

The Calendar

I GLANCED AT THE CLOCK on the wall in my kitchen, and the familiar whoosh of adrenaline flooded into my system. I had to get my three young teen kids to three different destinations at the same time, and we were running late. In other words, it was a typical Tuesday in our suburban household.

"Get a move on, you guys," I called, ratcheting up my voice half an octave so my three young teens would catch my sense of urgency. "We should have been out of here five minutes ago! Rachel, do you have your Spanish folder? Ben, where's your tie?"

Jacob yelled from the basement, "I'll be there in just a minute. I just have to finish—"

"No, not 'just a minute,' Jake," I interrupted him. "Now!"

Rachel stomped into the room. "I can't find my Spanish folder."

"Did you look in that pile of books by the piano?" She stomped out of the room in double time. On cue, Jacob emerged from the basement, no shoes or socks on his feet.

"I think all your socks are in the laundry," I told him. "You'll have to run back downstairs and grab a pair from the dirty pile. Hurry!"

From the living room, Rachel called, "I can't find my folder anywhere!"

At that moment, Jacob emerged from the basement holding an unmatched pair of tube socks as if he were carrying a sack of rabid bats. "*This* is the only pair I could find."

Ben clipped his tie onto his grocery store uniform shirt as he hustled past me to the car, muttering, "I'm gonna be late for work."

It's been more than a decade and a half since I was chauffeuring my kids around our local suburban solar system. I have plenty of cherished memories of them during those growing-up years, but precious few of those memories were made during the frantic daily chase to lessons, after-school jobs, get-togethers with friends, or youth group activities. Though there are certainly seasons of life that are busier than others, it is true in every stage that abundant activity does not equal abundant life.

Eugene Peterson's paraphrase of Matthew 11:28-30 captures Jesus' winsome invitation to each one of us:

> Are you tired? Worn out? Burned out on religion? Come to me. Get away with me and you'll recover your life. I'll show you how to take a real rest. Walk with me and work with me—watch how I do it. Learn the unforced rhythms of grace. I won't lay anything heavy or ill-fitting on you. Keep company with me and you'll learn to live freely and lightly. MATTHEW 11:28-30, MSG

A rhythm is by definition a pattern. Many of us get used to living without a pattern, without pauses or punctuation marks:

Our days bleed together *onetothenext*. Though penciling onto our calendars some breaks in the form of vacations, downtime, and appointments to gather with family and friends will create a little bit of emotional breathing room in our 24/7 lives, we still function as though we're the author of our stories. There's not much space for grace if that's the case.

Most of us in the church have heard plenty of messages about the generous use of our financial resources or the value of serving others with our gifts and talents. The way we use our time is often included in the way we talk about stewardship. Time is a precious, irreplaceable resource, certainly. But when we speak of it only in terms of something at our disposal, we risk missing much grander and more beautiful truths about ourselves and the One who made it for us.

IN THE BEGINNING...

The first words of Genesis 1 highlight the way in which the eternal God first chose to express himself as Creator. The words "in the beginning" establish a line of demarcation between the eternal One and his finite creation. He anchored time to a fixed point "in the beginning" in order to unfold the rest of his creation. Indeed, the notion of time itself speaks of limits. Time can be measured, a distinct contrast with the limitlessness of God.

Yet God reveals his own use of created time throughout Genesis 1. Each movement of creation ends with a time stamp: "There was evening, and there was morning—the first day . . . the second day . . . the third day"—all the way through to the description of the creation of Adam on the sixth day. Even on the final day of the creation week, the holy rest had a beginning, a middle, and an end.

The way in which time was lived and measured by the ancient Jews was extremely countercultural. Writer Thomas Cahill credits the God of the Jews with changing the way in which ancient peoples measured time. Every other ancient civilization (such as the Sumerians and Egyptians) saw time cycling continually in place, without a larger purpose. "Cyclical religion goes nowhere," he writes, "because, within its comprehension, there is no future as we have come to understand it, only the next revolution of the Wheel." The human race began to talk about time differently when God called Abram to leave Ur by faith and head to an unknown land God would show him. Cahill continues,

> *Since time is no longer cyclical but one-way and irreversible, personal history is now possible and an individual life can have value. This new value is at first hardly understood; but already in the earliest accounts of Avraham* [Abraham] *and his family we come upon the carefully composed genealogies of ordinary people, something it would have never occurred to Sumerians* [the dominant civilization in the region at the time Abram was living] *to write down, because they accorded no importance to individual memories.*[1]

Time became a journey, not a wheel. What's more, the journey had an eternal purpose—and a destination.

Within a few generations, Abraham's descendants eventually found their way to safe harbor in Egypt during a time of famine in the Promised Land. Within a few more generations, these honored guests of one pharaoh became slaves of another, who carried no memory of the blessing Abraham's great-grandson Joseph had been to the Egyptian people.

After four centuries of slavery, Moses led the people into the desert and then, after forty years of wandering, to the edge of home once again. As they traveled through time and place in God's company, they learned what it meant to stop living as refugees and begin living as pilgrims. The journey from slavery to freedom, from wandering to rootedness, and from seeing themselves as a family of tribes to embracing their calling as God's Chosen People occurred in the school of the desert. They'd known God as their Creator in Egypt, but by the time they crossed the Jordan River into the Promised Land, they'd learned that he was their Redeemer and Provider.

If you were to trace this journey on a map, it would form a ragged loop. But this loop doesn't represent the meaningless, repetitious, impersonal cycle of the pagan. This journey through time is, to use a New Testament term, a narrow path. It has a distinct beginning and a specific, holy destination.

Before they entered the Land, God emphasized once again that their lives with him would be formed both by their day-to-day labor and by receiving his gifts of rest, celebration, and reconnection. Leviticus 23 prescribes the weekly Sabbath and the yearly cycle of holy days. The Sabbath gave God's people a day of sanctified rest, designed to renew their relationship with him and one another. In addition, throughout the year, the community would celebrate six holy gatherings that anchored them in the story of God's redemption. As they received these gifts of time from the Eternal One, he empowered them to spread his light to the world he loved.

Relationships are forged from time together. The unique relationship between God and the Hebrew people has been indelibly imprinted by both everyday discipleship and the weekly/yearly festal cycle. The calendar has been integral in developing Jewish identity—an identity that has held the Chosen People through millennia of dispersion, oppression, and suffering. It reminded them of who (and whose) they were when it would have been far easier to forget and assimilate into the surrounding culture.

The effect of living in time differently than the prevailing culture has essential lessons for us today. Our personal schedules are not the extent of our identity. When we are focused on the mission of God and allow its story to determine the rhythms of our lives as a community, we proclaim to the world around us that our God is one and our Messiah is Lord—and all the little Caesars around us are not.

LEARNING THE WAY OF JESUS VIA THE CALENDAR

The Gospel of John opens with the words, "In the beginning," a direct reference to Genesis 1. John emphasizes Jesus' eternal, divine nature as Lord and Maker of his creation. In order to restore this creation to himself, Jesus maintained his divinity while at the same time choosing out of love to become a fully human member of his own creation: "The Word became flesh and made his dwelling among us" (John 1:14). In so doing, he placed himself amid the Hebrew community he'd called millennia earlier to reflect his light to the world. The Jewish Jesus grew up celebrating the holy days prescribed in the Law. As he stepped into his ministry years, Jesus applied to himself his heavenly Father's intention and meaning for those days in ways that confounded some of his listeners and caused others to draw near to God. Every time he healed on the day of rest, he reflected his Father's restorative purpose of the Sabbath (see Mark 3:1-6). He modeled the kind of actions that flow from a clean heart as he washed his disciples' feet during his last Passover meal with them

(John 13:1-7). And in his resurrection he showed us that eternal life was his gift to us in our here and now (Matthew 28; Mark 16; Luke 24; John 20).

On the first Shavuot (Pentecost) after his resurrection, Jesus' band of Jewish disciples became a body of more than three thousand people (Acts 2). They were first known as a sect of Judaism, followers of the Way (Acts 22:4). It was only as Gentiles flowed into the church over the following decades that a shift began to occur away from the Jewish cycle of marking time. Paul's words to his Gentile friends in Rome reflect the beginning of that shift:

> One person considers one day more sacred than another; another considers every day alike. Each of them should be fully convinced in their own mind. ROMANS 14:5

The apostle to the Gentiles was concerned for what motivated Gentiles to adhere to the festal cycle given to the Jews:

> Now that you know God—or rather are known by God—how is it that you are turning back to those weak and miserable forces? Do you wish to be enslaved by them all over again? You are observing special days and months and seasons and years! I fear for you, that somehow I have wasted my efforts on you. GALATIANS 4:9-11

But it's important to remember that the Jewish man who wrote these words himself continued to mark time by Jewish feasts, even as he spoke or wrote to primarily Gentile audiences (see Acts 20:16; 1 Corinthians 5:7; 16:8). Paul did not want to see those who'd been incarcerated in the prison of paganism continue to function as if they were captives—not after they'd been set gloriously free by Jesus the Messiah. Paul wanted them to remember that Jew and Gentile alike were free to live, celebrate, and proclaim God's salvation story.

Gentile Christians continued to grow in number, and in order to trace the story of their Savior through time each year, they adapted essential days from the Jewish calendar while also reimagining some of their own cultural festivals. The church calendar that took shape served as both a discipleship tool and missional "marching orders" for the Christian community. It was how the church learned what it means to walk in the way of Jesus. As such, this calendar mirrored the same message as the Jewish festal calendar from which it grew: You and I are not the center of the universe. It's really, truly not about us.

MEASURING TIME, BEING MEASURED BY TIME

The calendar used by a people shapes their culture. Calendars in all cultures mark big events and measure ordinary days as well. The Jewish people worshipped in time to the festal calendar and eventually came to use the festal calendar as the basis for their civil calendar.

The festal year was linked to agricultural seasons. The first month of the year, Nisan, is in early spring, but the Jewish civil year begins in the fall, on the first day of the seventh month of the year. Confusing? Consider the way in which we mark time in our own culture.

Our calendar tells us a new civil year begins on January 1. However, we also have an academic year, beginning in late August or early September. The academic year was set up as a way of standardizing public education in a way that reflected earlier agrarian rhythms and accommodated common cultural practices such as summertime travel that allowed families to escape the sweltering heat of congested cities.

The Jewish calendar was a lunar calendar. Each month traced the twenty-eight-day cycle of the moon. Several other ancient civilizations used a lunar calendar as well, but those calendars didn't reflect the belief of the Jews that they were on a pilgrimage through time with and toward God.

Because most of the first followers of Jesus were Jews, the lunar calendar shaped the worship of the early church. If you've ever wondered why we celebrate Easter on March 28 one year and April 15 on another, your answer is found in the lunar calendar: Passover, the holiday so linked to the crucifixion and resurrection of Jesus, is calculated from a lunar year of only about 355 days. (A "leap month" is added to the Hebrew calendar every few years so that the feasts remain aligned with their agricultural seasons.)[2]

Over the next centuries, for a host of reasons, the church moved to a solar calendar. Roman emperor Julius Caesar introduced this calendar about four decades before Jesus was born in an attempt to correct the discrepancy between the lunar cycles and our earth's 365-and-a-quarter-day annual trip around the sun. Christian celebrations such as Christmas were anchored in this Julian solar calendar. But the Julian calendar had its own issues with imprecision. The "movable feasts" of Easter and Pentecost (so named because they were tied to the lunar calendar and changed from year to year) had been drifting ever later in the calendar. So in AD 1582, Pope Gregory XIII (aided by mathematicians and astronomers) fine-tuned the Julian calendar. These adjustments included changing the way in which leap years are calculated and removing ten days from that year's calendar. Over time, the Gregorian calendar became the de facto civil calendar of the West, and today it is the primary tool by which much of the world plans its business meetings, date-stamps legal documents, and schedules piano lessons and work hours at the local grocery store.

Many of us treat the civil calendar as if it's a giant empty cabinet awaiting the details of our lives. We stock it with containers of appointments, boxes crammed full of work time, and stacks of recreational activity, acting in the process as though we're captains of our calendars. But this approach to the calendar more closely resembles that ancient, cyclical calendar in which there is no meaning in our past or future, only in the acquisitions and achievements of our present. There is no story, no journey associated with our civil calendar. We have to look elsewhere for that.

When we pray, "Teach us to number our days, that we may gain a heart of wisdom" (Psalm 90:12), we are not asking for a tidier organizational system for our calendars. Wisdom is not a clever squishing of time to fit daily Bible reading into our schedule or have better attendance at weekly worship services. The Chosen People discovered more than three millennia ago that when God called them to number their days, it wasn't about rearranging their calendar, but about reorienting their lives—heart, soul, mind, and strength—as they followed him like pilgrims through time.

PART ONE

Jewish Biblical and Historical Feasts

2

IN THE BEGINNING

Introduction to the Jewish Calendar

GENERATIONS OF SLAVERY had stolen their freedom from them. But it had also given the Hebrew people something they didn't know they possessed: the courage to follow God as he delivered them out of their miserable but predictable existence.

The people trusted Moses as he guided them out of slavery in Egypt, but that trust frayed and fizzled in the desert sun. As they were poised to enter the Promised Land, their spiritual mutiny brought God's discipline upon them: They'd wander the desert. Only after the original group of slaves had died in the wilderness, save Joshua and Caleb, would the Chosen People at last come home to the place God had led their forebear, Abraham, more than four hundred years earlier.

There was absolutely no reason for the people, who'd been led out of Egypt by miracle after miracle, to mistrust God. This mistrust blossomed into sin and kept them from fully realizing God's promise of a return home. Moses' unbelief, which erupted in a moment of anger when he disobeyed a direct command from God, brought him under the same sentence of discipline. He led his people through forty years in the desert while the generation of those enslaved in Egypt died in the wilderness. The children of those slaves were shaped by their parents' stories and God's promise, presence, and provision each day in the desert.

Moses was eighty when he led his people out of slavery into freedom. He died forty years after that. It was this man who prayed, "Teach us to number our days, that we may gain a heart of wisdom" (Psalm 90:12). He watched as one after another died, knowing that he would lead their children to the edge and that this would complete his mission. It is easy to miss the urgency in Moses' plea. The New Living Translation helps us hear it: "Teach us to realize the brevity of life."

Pastor Tom Olson said, "Learning to number our days means recognizing the unnumbered days of God."[1] By affirming that he is eternal, we are freed to come to terms with our own limitations. We are finite creatures, locked in time. A wise life is forged from the choices we make to follow God moment by moment.

Deuteronomy 6:4-9 speaks to this moment-by-moment discipleship. This Scripture passage is foundational for the Jewish people; religiously observant Jews pray these words twice daily. These words have shaped their experience of what it looks like to grow daily in the knowledge of God and to pass his wisdom on to the next generation:

> Hear, O Israel: The LORD our God, the LORD is one. Love the LORD your God with all your heart and with all your soul and with all your strength. These commandments that I give you today are to be on your hearts. Impress them on your children. Talk about them when you sit at home and when you walk along the road, when you lie

down and when you get up. Tie them as symbols on your
hands and bind them on your foreheads. Write them on
the doorframes of your houses and on your gates.

From the beginning of the story, God wanted his people to
know that every day was not the same. He did so first by modeling
and sanctifying the weekly pattern of six days of work and a day of
rest; God himself rested on the seventh day, then set apart the day
as a gift to his creation (Genesis 2:3). He then gave his people a
way to learn his story and theirs through a yearly cycle of holy days.
When God gave the Law to Moses at Sinai, it was far more than a
list of dos and don'ts. It was a way to commune in time with the
One who revealed himself as "I AM," eternally existing beyond time.

INHABITING ETERNITY

Understanding the Jewish calendar begins with the setting of
the sun. For the Jew, this is when a new day begins. This way of
metering out a day comes from the first movement of the creation
account: After God separated the day's light from the nighttime
darkness, Scripture tells us, "There was evening, and there was
morning—the first day" (Genesis 1:5).

This view of time informed Jewish identity. Moving from darkness to light daily underscored and affirmed their unique calling
and mission. God had called them to be a kingdom of priests,
reflecting his light to the nations (Deuteronomy 7:7-8; see also
Isaiah 42:6; 49:6; 60:3).

Months in the Jewish calendar are measured by the moon.
The lunar calendar's rhythm of work and rest, ordinary days and
festivals, was a sort of school in which they were enrolled from
birth to death. Jewish identity was shaped by the sundown days,

the Sabbath-punctuated weeks, the new-moon months, and the yearly rhythms of corporate worship feasts and fasts. Rabbi Samson Raphael Hirsch once noted, "The Jew's calendar is his catechism."[2] This calendar was the primary way in which the entire community lived out God's command to pass on the faith from one generation to the next. Abraham Joshua Heschel wrote,

> *While the deities of other peoples were associated with places or things, the God of Israel was the God of events: the Redeemer from slavery, the Revealer of the Torah [the Law given to Moses at Mt. Sinai and contained in the first five books of the Old Testament], manifesting Himself in events of history rather than in things or places. . . . Judaism is a* religion of time *aiming at the* sanctification of time. *"*[3]

We moderns view time as something to be measured. In ancient days, the Chosen People experienced time as a realm they inhabited.[4]

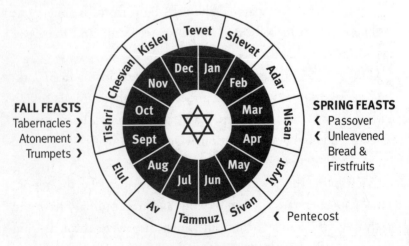

Figure 1. The Jewish lunar calendar

LEARNING AND RELEARNING THE STORY OF SALVATION

The realm of time was marked for the Hebrew people by the temporal measures of days, weeks, and months. However, time was defined by seeing themselves as part of God's eternal story. As they participated in specific appointed times to meet with God throughout each year, they immersed themselves afresh in his story of creation, redemption, and re-creation. These holy appointments were tied to the agricultural year, which underscored the role of God as provider to the people. Leviticus 23 lists the times the Israelites were called to pause their regularly scheduled daily activities in order to worship God as a community. Along with the weekly Sabbath (Leviticus 23:3), each of the six spring and fall festivals included rest days, during which no

Spring Festivals	Fall Festivals
Passover (a pilgrim feast) The beginning of the festal year, this day commemorates God's deliverance of the Israelites through the blood of a perfect lamb the night the plague of death came to the firstborn of the Egyptians (Exodus 12:1-30).	*Rosh Hashanah/Feast of Trumpets* This early fall holiday is a call to repentance and honors God as both Creator and King of all. Coming at the beginning of the seventh month of the Jewish calendar, it functioned as the launch point of the new civil (business, government) year.
Feast of Unleavened Bread and First Fruits A continuation of the Passover story, this seven-day holiday officially begins the day after the Passover feast. During this period, the people abstain from all food containing leaven in obedience to God's command to eat unleavened bread in memory of their hasty departure from Egypt (Exodus 12:15-20).	*Yom Kippur/Day of Atonement* The most sacred day of the entire year, this is when the high priest would enter the Holy of Holies to make atonement for the sins of the people.
Shavuot/Pentecost (a pilgrim feast) Fifty days after Passover, this holy day marked the end of the harvest season. It has also come to commemorate the day God gave the Law at Mount Sinai.	*Sukkot/Feast of Tabernacles (a pilgrim feast)* Sukkot refers to the individual tents, or booths, that sheltered the Chosen People in the wilderness. This joyous harvest holiday is filled with the expression of longing for a Messiah who will dwell with his people forever.

Table 1. The appointed feasts and holy days of Leviticus 23.

work was permitted. Three of these holidays, known as the pilgrim feasts, required the people to leave their homes and gather as one.

After the Chosen People found a home in the Promised Land at the end of forty years of wandering, God called them to remember he'd fed them for more than fourteen thousand desert days while leading them to abundant provision, as he'd promised (Exodus 3:16-17). Their desert sojourn may have come to an end, but God wanted his people to remember they'd always be spiritual pilgrims.

In addition to the holy days God named in the Torah, over time the Jewish festal cycle expanded to include a number of other important historical days of celebration and mourning. Some of these have more prominence in popular culture than the feasts mandated by Scripture. For example, though Chanukah is a minor holiday, many people imagine it is something like a Jewish Christmas because it is usually celebrated during the month of December. Holocaust Remembrance Day events may net a mention in your local newspaper, but rarely will Sukkot get a similar write-up.

The modern Jewish community has differing levels of observance of these holy days, depending on the individual's or family's level of everyday religious involvement. For example, though my own family wasn't especially religious when I was growing up, we always observed Passover, Rosh Hashanah, Yom Kippur, and Chanukah—my childhood favorite. (The presents I received for eight nights of every December may have had something to do with that.)

THE SEVEN HOLY DAYS JESUS OBSERVED

Every single year the biblical feasts illumine God's character and invite participants into the salvation story afresh. Jesus himself

Tu B'Shvat Leviticus 19:23-35 details the laws regarding how many years had to pass before the fruit of a young tree could be eaten. This midwinter holiday is known as the new year for trees, as it is when the trees in Israel begin budding.	January/ February
Purim Esther's beauty and bravery and help from her cousin Mordecai combined to save her people from an ancient holocaust during the time of the Babylonian exile, six centuries before the birth of Christ.	February/ March
Yom HaShoah/Holocaust Remembrance Day This recent addition to the Jewish calendar cycle gives the Jewish community a time to mourn the loss of six million Jewish lives at the hands of Nazi Germany during World War II.	April/May
Tisha B'Av This day of fasting and mourning commemorates the destruction of the first and second Temples in 586 BC and AD 70, respectively. This date on the Jewish calendar is also the date that a number of other catastrophes have befallen the Jewish people throughout history.	July/ August
Chanukah Chanukah celebrates the account of the Jewish Maccabees fighting to reclaim and rededicate the Temple in Jerusalem more than a century and a half before Jesus was born. This story is found in the apocryphal books of 1–2 Maccabees and is not included in either Jewish or Protestant Bibles.	November/ December

Table 2. Additional days of celebration and mourning on the Jewish calendar.

observed the Sabbath and festal days prescribed by God in the Torah. By getting to know the Jewish feasts, we get to know our Jewish Savior better.

The spring festivals point to the redemption story fulfilled by the wholly human, completely divine Son of God, born miraculously to Mary in Bethlehem and discipled, Deuteronomy 6:4-9 style, by his earthly father, Joseph, in Nazareth. He ministered throughout Galilee, was crucified in Jerusalem during the Passover feast, and was resurrected on the third day. Jesus entirely realized the story of the spring feasts with his life, death, and resurrection. After the Resurrection, he gave his ministry to his disciples, spelling out what their work would be until his return:

He said to them, "This is what I told you while I was
still with you: Everything must be fulfilled that is written
about me in the Law of Moses, the Prophets and the
Psalms."

Then he opened their minds so they could understand
the Scriptures. He told them, "This is what is written:
The Messiah will suffer and rise from the dead on the
third day, and repentance for the forgiveness of sins
will be preached in his name to all nations, beginning
at Jerusalem. You are witnesses of these things."
LUKE 24:44-48

For the Jews, the fall feasts are rich with the promise of a
peace-filled future ruled by a Messiah from the lineage of David.
Christians recognize the Messiah's name as Jesus. The fall holy days
point with precision to a future fulfillment: Jesus, descended from
the line of King David (see 2 Samuel 7:8-16; Luke 3:23-38), will
return to the earth in revealed majesty (see Revelation 19:11-16).
He spoke of his return throughout his earthly ministry and was
crucified with the title "King of the Jews" hammered to the cross
(Luke 23:38). The author of Hebrews makes clear his plan to
return:

He has appeared once for all at the culmination of the
ages to do away with sin by the sacrifice of himself. Just
as people are destined to die once, and after that to face
judgment, so Christ was sacrificed once to take away the
sins of many; and he will appear a second time, not to
bear sin, but to bring salvation to those who are waiting
for him. HEBREWS 9:26-28

WHAT DO JEWISH PEOPLE BELIEVE ABOUT JESUS?

Only a very small percentage of Jewish people believe that Jesus is the Messiah promised in the Old Testament. Many in the Jewish community will affirm that Jesus was a great rabbi, or teacher. But generations of Jews suffering at the hands of Gentiles who called themselves "Christians" (as was common during the medieval Inquisition and during the Holocaust), as well as a horrifying history of anti-Semitism, persecution, and forced expulsions from various countries in Europe, North Africa, the Middle East, and Russia, have not provided a winsome witness, to put it mildly.

There may be between six and seven million Jews in the United States.[5] The Jewish community in America is about 10 percent Orthodox (very observant, usually concentrated in urban or suburban communities), 26 percent Conservative (still observant, but with more flexible rules and a more relaxed approach to contemporary culture), and 35 percent Reform (a more liberal or humanist approach to Jewish practice and ethics).[6] A significant percentage of American Jews do not identify with any one of these three streams of practice, and many of these unaffiliated, secular people maintain Jewish ethnic identity while functioning as agnostics or atheists.[7] Some have estimated that there are as many as one hundred thousand Messianic Jews in the United States— some worshipping among one of two hundred to three hundred Messianic congregations, with others worshipping in a local, traditionally Christian church.[8]

Throughout the next seven chapters, when I talk about Jesus, offer New Testament insight, or quote Christian writers, I am doing so because I want to help my Gentile brothers and sisters to know the amazing riches of the family story into which they've been adopted. Most Jewish people do not (yet) believe in Jesus as

Messiah, but what you discover in the coming pages may change the way you pray for and relate to a Jewish person you know. (The appendixes at the end of this book can provide you with additional tools.)

The story of God's faithful engagement of his Chosen People through times of trouble and times of expansion, and the mission that God invited those Chosen People into through the celebration of these feasts and holy days, may change the way you choose to live the moments and days of your life, too.

3

DAY OF YES, DAY OF REST

The Sabbath

I ONCE SERVED as a writing tutor for groups of middle school and high school students. In order to illustrate for them the way a single word can carry a variety of shadings of meaning, I would ask each student to write a quick description of the first image of a dog that popped into their minds. They would paint word pictures of overweight beagles, fierce pit bulls, high-strung poodles, or their family's beloved mutt. One single word—*dog*—conjured a kennel full of different images. Four legs, wagging tails, and wet noses come in a lot of different shapes and sizes.

The word *Sabbath* is a little bit like this. What is the first image that comes to your mind when you read it? I've found that the word conjures a variety of images, including

› Orthodox Jewish people choosing not to light their stoves or flip the light switches in their homes on or off from just before sundown on Friday to just after sundown on Saturday;

> Amish and Old Order Mennonites and Brethren driving their horse-drawn buggies to biweekly, all-day Sunday church meetings;
> Colonial-era Puritans spending sober Sundays in hours-long church meetings, followed by hours of sitting quietly and stoically at home;
> secular self-help gurus telling us we need to practice good self-care by unplugging from our electronics on a weekly basis; and
> weekends spent catching up on chores or ferrying the kids to their soccer or Little League games.

Most of these images paint the Sabbath as a day of "no," in which religious rules bring everyday life to a screeching halt. Our plugged-in, always-on culture certainly has no space for what appears to be an irrelevant, weekly historical relic. For others, the idea of Sabbath is attendance at a church service followed by a meal with family or friends and an afternoon watching sports on TV or doing yard work. At best, this list gives us the notion of Sabbath as "me time," a minivacation to maintain our emotional balance.

Sabbath observance has set the Jews apart from every culture in which they've lived. Throughout history, it has led to persecution. Two millennia ago, Jewish slaves were punished by their Roman rulers for refusing to work on Shabbat. During the late Middle Ages, when Jews in Spain were forced at swordpoint to "convert" to Catholicism, many of these *conversos* continued to gather in secret to observe Shabbat. And in the twentieth century, Jews were punished harshly in the Soviet Union because they wouldn't work on Shabbat. Though Sabbath-keeping has come at a very high cost for the Jewish people, religiously observant Jews understood that this was a nonnegotiable part of their identity as People of the Book, called to be a light to the nations (Isaiah 49:6). As writer Ahad Ha'am is often quoted, "More than the Jewish people have kept the Sabbath, the Sabbath has kept the Jews."

REST

Though Sabbath is often framed in the negative (no work), it is better thought of as God's yes to us. Sabbath has a place in the Word of God from the very beginning: "By the seventh day God had finished the work he had been doing; so on the seventh day *he rested* from all his work. Then God blessed the seventh day and made it holy, because on it *he rested* from all the work of creating that he had done" (Genesis 2:2-3, emphasis added). The word *rest—shabbat—*doesn't mean God needed a long, restorative nap in his heavenly La-Z-Boy. *Shabbat* tells us God ceased his normal activity in order to bring about something else. This rest was a life-giving blessing to his beloved creation. As Rabbi Abraham Joshua Heschel notes,

> *The meaning of the Sabbath is to celebrate time rather than space. Six days a week we live under the tyranny of things and space; on the Sabbath we try to become attuned to holiness in time. It is a day on which we are called upon to share in what is eternal in time, to turn from the results of creation to the mystery of creation; from the world of creation to the creation of the world.*[1]

After God delivered the Hebrew people from their enslavement in Egypt, we see a reminder of God's temporal rhythm of time in the instructions Moses gave about how to gather the manna that would sustain the people during their desert journey. God would provide manna six days a week. On the sixth day, he would give double the amount because there would be none on the Sabbath (Exodus 16:21-30). It was a rhythm with which the people were acquainted, at least via the stories of their forebears, as it is highly unlikely they'd had a day of rest during their years of enslavement (Exodus 5:1-20).

The Sabbath is the fourth of the Ten Commandments:

> Remember the Sabbath day by keeping it holy. Six days
> you shall labor and do all your work, but the seventh day
> is a sabbath to the LORD your God. On it you shall not
> do any work, neither you, nor your son or daughter, nor
> your male or female servant, nor your animals, nor any
> foreigner residing in your towns. For in six days the LORD
> made the heavens and the earth, the sea, and all that is
> in them, but he rested on the seventh day. Therefore the
> LORD blessed the Sabbath day and made it holy.
>
> EXODUS 20:8-11

The first four commandments speak of the ways in which we are to love and honor God. The remaining six describe the ways in which we are to treat others. Though the fourth commandment highlights the fact that the Sabbath is a day set apart for God, he invites his beloved creation into communion with him and one another on this weekly holy day. "The Sabbath rest is for all of God's creation, and reveals the idea of social equality under the rule of the LORD," writes scholar John Parsons. "No one is excluded from this blessing, including your children, your servants, your animals, or converts to the faith. There is no second-class citizenry in relation to being part of the created order."[2] Once a week, the entire community was to do exactly the same thing—together. What they did on that day each week was a lot of "not doing": no work save that of the worship that flowed from receiving the gifts of rest, restoration, and renewal from God.

The notion of Sabbath rest in Israel extended to seven-year cycles in which farmers were required to give their land a yearly rest and creditors were expected to forgive the debts they were owed. At the end of seven of those seven-year cycles, a Jubilee year served as a Sabbath celebration for the nation, when land was to lie fallow for a year and those who'd sold themselves into slavery to pay debts would be set free (Leviticus 25–26). The Sabbath principle permeated the Hebrew understanding of time and extended it beyond individual families or the community. Sabbatical years and the Jubilee affected relationships with tribal and national neighbors. Instead of war or treaties as a means by which justice could be achieved with those neighbors, Israel was called to trust God, relinquish her "rights" to restoration, and wipe the slate clean. While it is unclear how often ancient Israel actually fully practiced national Sabbatical or Jubilee years, the fact that they're embedded in the Torah points to the profound way in which the Sabbath shaped the Jewish understanding of time.

NOT QUITE PARADISE: EXILE AND FENCES

Deuteronomy 28 lists the blessings God would pour out on Israel as they obeyed his Law and the consequences (curses) that would follow if they didn't. One of the curses included uprooting from their homes and land and dispersion among the nations. As a consequence, the people would not experience God's rest:

> Among those nations you will find no repose, no resting
> place for the sole of your foot. There the LORD will give
> you an anxious mind, eyes weary with longing, and a
> despairing heart.   DEUTERONOMY 28:65

The Old Testament often portrays a beloved but rebellious Israel doing all she could to become just like all the other nations in the neighborhood. That compromise came at a high cost. Fraught with internal power struggles and idolatry, Israel divided into a northern and a southern kingdom, each with its own government. In approximately 720 BC, the Assyrians conquered the northern kingdom, taking some Israelites into captivity and forcing the others to scatter. The southern kingdom, which contained the people of the tribes of Judah and Benjamin, hung on a little longer but was conquered by the Babylonians in 586 BC. Solomon's Temple in Jerusalem was destroyed, and many of the nation's people were marched across the Fertile Crescent into captivity in Babylon.

What happened while the people were in captivity was a turning point in the way in which the Chosen People observed the Sabbath. They could no longer observe the Temple-focused feasts in the way God had prescribed them; they could maintain their Jewish identity only by continuing to circumcise their baby boys (Genesis 17) and by their Sabbath observance. These spiritual markers of identity grew in importance during the years in which the Hebrew people were in captivity.

Seventy years later, Persian King Cyrus the Great miraculously permitted groups to return to Jerusalem to rebuild the Temple and surrounding city. The books of Ezra and Nehemiah detail the return and spiritual reboot that occurred during this period.

Nehemiah's reverence for the Lord and the Sabbath observance he'd learned in Babylon combined in a confrontation with those who were conducting business on the holy day. Nehemiah locked the gates surrounding Jerusalem in advance of Shabbat each week, ensuring that the people would keep the Sabbath whether they wanted to or not (Nehemiah 13:19-22).

In the same vein as Nehemiah's action, Jewish religious leaders began adding protective layers of rules to the laws God had given to his people. A "fence around the Torah" (*gezerah*) was designed to protect people from inadvertently breaking a commandment. In the case of the Sabbath, the simplicity of God's command not to do any work expanded by an ever-more complex and specific maze of *gezerot*. Over the next five hundred years, Sabbath observance was attacked from without (as surrounding nations used the Jews' enforced day of rest to their own advantage in military conflicts) and from within (as the Jewish people struggled to find respite among the ever-more-oppressive and restrictive rules).

JESUS THE SABBATH KEEPER

When Jesus said, "The Sabbath was made for man, not man for the Sabbath. So the Son of Man is Lord even of the Sabbath" (Mark 2:27-28), he was proclaiming good news to people who'd perhaps nearly forgotten that the point of the day of rest wasn't about coloring within the fence lines. Jesus confronted the unnecessary *gezerot* while simultaneously fulfilling with his words and works his Father's eternal intent and meaning for this weekly festal day.

Luke 4:14-30 recounts Jesus teaching on Shabbat in a Nazareth synagogue. He'd grown up in that town, learning obedience in all things through the six-days-of-work, one-day-of-rest rhythm of Jewish life. He maintained those rhythms throughout his life and upheld them perfectly through his death and resurrection (Matthew 28:1; Mark 15:42-43; Mark 16:1; Luke 23:50-56; John 19:31).

Jesus did works of mercy and healing on the Sabbath. These included

> › advocating for his disciples as they plucked heads of grain for food (Matthew 12:1-8);
> › healing a man with a withered hand (Mark 3:1-6);
> › bringing deliverance to a crippled, oppressed woman (Luke 13:10-17);
> › restoring health to a man suffering from abnormal swelling (Luke 14:1-6);
> › healing a crippled man at the pool of Bethesda (John 5:1-18); and
> › giving vision to a man born blind (John 9:1-16).

When Jesus scaled the fences of *gezerot* around the good boundary of Shabbat rest, it was to show us what rest was meant to be: restoration, recreation, renewal, redemption, and reunion with one another and with the Triune One. Shabbat simultaneously pointed backward to the first day in Eden and forward to the final day when all of creation will find wholeness and rest in unbroken fellowship with God.

One Shabbat, a religious leader confronted Jesus after Jesus healed a woman who'd been crippled for eighteen years by an oppressing spirit. The illogic of the leader's words would be funny if they weren't as serious as a heart attack. "Indignant because Jesus had healed on the Sabbath, the synagogue leader said to the people, 'There are six days for work. So come and be healed on those days, not on the Sabbath'" (Luke 13:14).

In his zeal for a fenced-in Sabbath, the synagogue leader had moved miles away from what the day was meant to be. Jesus knew the synagogue leaders had made provision in the *gezerot* so they could "work" on Shabbat to feed and water their livestock. He pointed out the hypocrisy of rules that would provide humane care for animals but not allow for mercy and restoration to be given to a suffering woman (Luke 13:15-16).

Jesus maintained the true integrity and intent of the Sabbath through his life and even in the timing of his death and resurrection. He was crucified before the beginning of the Sabbath and resurrected after the Sabbath had concluded. Jesus not only fulfilled God's intention for the Sabbath but also became our Sabbath.

The writer of the letter to the Hebrews was addressing an audience of first-century Jewish followers of Jesus when he wrote, "There remains, then, a Sabbath-rest for the people of God; for anyone who enters God's rest also rests from their works, just as God did from his" (Hebrews 4:9-10). Protestant believers often hear in the word *works* the notion of doing good things to gain merit in God's sight, but the Greek word used in this verse is *ergon*, which includes any act of creation on our part. Entering into the Sabbath rest to which Jesus is inviting us means we receive what has been done for us by Jesus. We drop the works our hands are clutching and surrender our empty hands to receive the abundant life he offers us.

Sabbath rest is characterized by our state of shalom with him. The word *shalom* is a Hebrew greeting, a word for peace, but it carries the imprint of eternity. One of my favorite definitions for the word comes from theologian Cornelius Plantinga:

In the Bible, shalom means universal flourishing, wholeness, and delight—a rich state of affairs in which natural needs are satisfied and natural gifts fruitfully employed, a state of affairs that inspires joyful wonder as its Creator and Savior opens doors and welcomes the creatures in whom He delights. Shalom, in other words, is the way things ought to be.[3]

THE FORK IN THE ROAD

Initially and throughout much of the first century, most of Jesus' followers were Jewish, and the ever-growing group was recognized as a sect within Judaism. Exponential growth in the numbers of Gentile followers of Jesus across Asia and the Mediterranean basin, however, forced early church leaders to figure out how to facilitate fellowship between former Gentile pagans and Jewish believers. It is worth noting that Sabbath keeping by the Gentiles was not on the list of basic requirements for fellowship (Acts 15:28-29). Further, there is scant evidence in the early years of the church that there was ever a Shabbat versus Sunday worship debate.

However, the destruction of the Temple in Jerusalem in AD 70 exacerbated the growing divide between the Jewish community and the young Christian community. After Roman Emperor Hadrian's troops had driven the Jews from Jerusalem by AD 73, Jewish religious leaders applied the lessons they'd learned more than five hundred years earlier in Babylon to maintain Jewish identity. Without the Temple as a focal point for worship, practices of piety shaped the faith expression of the Jewish diaspora (dispersed peoples) from that time until today. It turns out those *gezerot* were portable, and they contributed to Israel's continued existence.

The first- and second-century church increasingly sought to differentiate itself from its Jewish foundations. On March 3, 321,

Constantine decreed Sunday was now the official day of rest across the empire. Author Rich Robinson saw Constantine's law as "a secular, not theological, institution. No theological reasons were given for Sunday's becoming a rest day; it appears to have been just a practical and political move. But his law began to shape Sunday along the lines that it still has today."[4] The first day of the week had effectively become the "Christian Sabbath."

SABBATH PRAYER

The 1971 movie *Fiddler on the Roof* has a scene that captures what for observant Jews has been and continues to be the high point of the week: the beginning of the weekly Shabbat. In the film, Mama Golde kindles the Sabbath candles, and the family gathers around a holiday table as sunset approaches on Friday night. She and her milkman husband, Tevye, sing the poignant song "Sabbath Prayer." The head of the household blesses those gathered around the table for the festive, sacred meal.

While Shabbat observance is a commandment, how it is obeyed and practiced varies from community to community and family to family in the Jewish community. However, the cornerstones of a traditional Shabbat often include practices that would have been familiar to Tevye and Golde:

› Just before sundown, the women of the household kindle at least two candles. The candles symbolize the two imperatives of the Fourth Commandment: to remember and to sanctify. The candle lighting must take place before the sun sets and the prohibition against doing any sort of work (such as lighting a fire) comes into effect.

› Those gathered give thanks for the wine and challah (braided egg bread). There are normally two loaves of bread, a reminder of the double portion of manna God provided to his children in the wilderness.

› The male head of the household prays a blessing on his sons ("May God make you like Ephraim and Manasseh," Genesis 48:20) and daughters ("May you be like Sarah, Rebekah, Rachel, and Leah"). He then prays over his wife the words of the *Eshet Chayil* ("eh-SHET khay-IL"), the prayer formed from Proverbs 31:10-31 describing a woman of valor.

› The best meal of the week is then served.

› Some go to their synagogue on Friday evening for a prayer service. Others spend their Friday evening time in conversation around the table with family and invited guests.

› Many families awaken Saturday morning, eat a cold breakfast, then head to synagogue for another service, this time featuring Torah readings as well as additional readings from other portions of Scripture.

› On Saturday afternoon, family and guests share the third meal of Shabbat. In many communities, it is a slow-cooked, casserole-type dish that was prepared on Friday afternoon. Some families hold the dish in a low oven; others precook the dish and wrap it well in order to maintain its temperature. The day passes in leisurely rest and conversation.

› After three stars appear in the sky after sunset on Saturday, the family gathers for a *Havdalah* ("hahv-DA-luh"), or "separation," ceremony. A braided candle is lit as a way to mark the passing of another Sabbath. A box of sweet spices is passed from person to person as a way to savor the sweetness of the departed day of rest. Those gathered give thanks over a cup of wine, and each person takes a sip. The Havdalah candle is extinguished in the remaining wine, signaling the end of the Sabbath. A new week officially begins.

EVERYDAY ETERNITY: SABBATH

Author Lauren Winner was an Orthodox Jew before she came to faith in Jesus as a young adult. In her book *Mudhouse Sabbath*, she recounts a Sunday afternoon spent reading, writing, and sipping a hot chai in the Mudhouse Coffeehouse after attending a church service. She struggles with the disconnect between what Shabbat once was in her life and what it was (or wasn't) now:

> *What, really, was wrong with my Mudhouse Sabbath? After all, I did spend Sunday morning in church. And I wasn't working that afternoon, not exactly.*
>
> *A fine few hours, except that my Sunday was more an afternoon off than a Sabbath. It was an add-on to a busy week, not the fundamental unit around which I organized my life. The Hebrew word for* holy *means, literally, "set apart." In failing to live a Sabbath truly distinct from weekly time, I had violated a most basic command: to keep the Sabbath holy. . . .*
>
> *There is something in the Jewish Sabbath that is absent from most Christian Sundays: a true cessation from the rhythms of work and world, a time wholly set apart, and, perhaps above all, a sense that the point of Shabbat, the orientation of Shabbat, is toward God.*[5]

If we're having any conversations in church at all about what it means to keep and be kept by the Sabbath, those conversations tend to be framed in terms of individualistic self-care or an insistence that Sabbath keeping is a legalistic throwback that we're now free in Christ to dismiss.

Winner's words remind me that we're also free to *receive* Sabbath as the gift it was always intended to be. Viewing it in that light will change the kinds of conversations we are (and aren't) having about it. Conversation can lead to prayer, further study of the Scriptures, and perhaps a commitment to begin taking some small steps toward a Sabbath practice. In our 24/7 world, Sabbath keeping is something of a lost art.

A good starting point from which to confront our culture's insistence that we're always to be plugged in and productive is by considering that the Sabbath is a way to reclaim, express, and rest in your identity as a beloved member of God's family. By placing a stake in your calendar each week, you're doing more than mentally assenting to this truth. You're acting on it.

I suggest starting small. A good first step for some might be to unplug from technology once a week. Others might find it meaningful to block out time on a Friday or Saturday evening to gather with family or friends for a special Sabbath meal. Light some candles. Relax. Laugh! Thank God for his good gifts in your life. It's not the formality of the ritual that is most important when it comes to forming a Sabbath habit in your life; it's the commitment to rest with God.

Because God designed the Sabbath to be shared in community, a congregation gathering to study and prayerfully discuss the topic of the Sabbath is another good starting place. What might it look like for your church to invite the congregation into Sabbath rest while emphasizing that God has placed no *gezerot* around the Sabbath?

There is, simply, the yes of an open door and a place to rest with our Creator and one another.

4

INTO FREEDOM

Passover, Unleavened Bread, First Fruits

I ONCE ASKED A GROUP of elementary-age students what they understood about Communion. One girl piped up, "Communion is a little snack we have at church sometimes."

My raised eyebrows elicited a round of the standard Sunday School answers from the rest of the class: "It's about Jesus." Knowing where Communion comes from and how it is indeed all about Jesus connects us to the story of God's redemption in very profound ways. And that story begins with Passover.

Though Bible readers turn to Exodus 1 to begin reading the account of God's miraculous deliverance of the Hebrew people from slavery in Egypt, the story has its preamble in Genesis 37, when Joseph's brothers sold him into slavery. Trace the story through the rest of Genesis, and you'll read the remarkable account of how the dysfunctional clan was reunited in Egypt after more than two decades. Within a few short generations, the clan had gone from seventy honored guests of one pharaoh to a growing tribe of slaves under another pharaoh (see Exodus 1:12-14). This shouldn't have been a total surprise to the people: God had told Joseph's great-grandfather Abraham that his descendants would be enslaved for four hundred years (Genesis 15:13-14). However, the words got buried in the misery of dawn-to-dusk, seven-days-a-week forced labor.

Until Moses. He'd been spared from the decree of Pharaoh that all Israelite baby boys should be put to death in order to control the growth of the population (Exodus 1:15–2:10). In an incredible example of God's divine provision for his people, Moses became a member of the royal household during his childhood, the adopted son of one of Pharaoh's daughters. Moses eventually killed a man and left Egypt a fugitive, settling in Midian for years until he found himself before the presence of God. In the form of a burning-but-not-consumed bush in the desert, God spoke to Moses and sent him back to Egypt in order to lead his people to freedom.

When Moses first went to Pharaoh, he asked that the Israelites be permitted to worship their God in the wilderness for three days. Pharaoh's response to the request was to exponentially increase the workload of the slaves. To put it mildly, the people weren't too overjoyed with Moses.

When Moses questioned God about this strategy, the Lord let him know that out of this conflict, the Israelites and Egyptians alike would learn that there was no other God except him. He promised to bring his people into freedom by his own hand.

First, God sent the Chosen People to school. They had a national identity, but they needed to learn for themselves who their God was. They watched as Moses confronted one Egyptian false god after another with God's power through a series of plagues. Yet Pharaoh would not relent and set his captive workforce free, so in a final demonstration of his supremacy, the one true God struck down the firstborn children and livestock of the Egyptian people.

God gave Moses instructions that would spare the Israelites (and any Egyptians who chose to join them in obedience) from this horror. These instructions included slaying a spotless lamb and applying its blood to the doorposts of their homes. They would be consecrating their own firstborn children to the Lord and thus saving them from death.

On the night of this final plague in Egypt, the Israelites prepared *matzo*—unleavened bread—as a reminder that they'd be asked to leave Egypt in haste. They also ate bitter herbs as a reminder of the bitterness of their slave status.

During the night, every single Egyptian household discovered their firstborn children and livestock had been struck dead (Exodus 12:29-30). Pharaoh sent for Moses and his brother, Aaron, and at last permitted them to leave. Scripture notes that there were about six hundred thousand men in the company, plus women, children, livestock, and "many other people" (Exodus 12:38)— those Egyptians who'd chosen to honor the God of the Israelites.

Despite—or perhaps because of—the loss of his firstborn son, Pharaoh's hard heart took one more icy turn as he reconsidered his decision to send the Israelites away. He sent his army into the desert after them. God told Moses to raise his staff, the sign of the spiritual authority God had granted to him, and lead his people through the Red (Reed) Sea. God parted the waters, and the company processed through the walls of water on dry land. As Pharaoh's army went after them, the waters surged back to their normal state. Not a single Egyptian survived.

This supernatural story of deliverance is the story that has been told and retold for more than three millennia by the Jewish people through the spring feasts of Passover, Unleavened Bread, and First Fruits. These holy days mark the beginning of the festival year for the Jewish people. Leviticus 23:4-14 describes how God asked his people to observe these festal days:

> *Passover* began at sundown on the fourteenth day of the Hebrew springtime month of Nisan. This is when the ceremonial meal and retelling of the story was to occur.
> The *Feast of Unleavened Bread* began the next day, on the fifteenth day of Nisan, and lasted for seven days. During this time, the people were to eat only matzo and present offerings to the Lord. The first and last days of this feast were Sabbaths calling the people together to worship God and bring offerings. On the first night of this feast, a fifty-day "count up" to the next major feast began.
> The *Feast of First Fruits* occurred on the sixteenth day of Nisan. After arriving in the Promised Land, the Israelites were to bring before God the cream of the new crop of barley along with other offerings.

Most people now refer to this grouping of holy days as Passover. The Passover is at the core of Jewish identity, and this first pilgrim feast is a stunning account of God's saving, preserving power.

WHY IS THIS NIGHT DIFFERENT FROM ALL OTHER NIGHTS?

Before Passover begins, each household gets rid of all products that contain yeast or other leavening agents. After a thorough search and cleansing (the original "spring cleaning"!), food products containing leaven are burned, donated, or sold to Gentiles.

God commanded his people to eat only unleavened bread during Passover as a reminder of the hurried way in which they fled Egypt (Exodus 12:34-39; Deuteronomy 16:3). Scripture sometimes associates leaven with sin and decay. For instance, only unleavened grain offerings could be presented on the altar in the Old Testament (Leviticus 2:11; 6:17). Leaven leads to decomposition; thus, it would render a grain offering impure. Jesus and Paul both built on this understanding when each used the idea of leaven as a symbol of things that decay relationship with God (Matthew 16:6-12; Mark 8:14-21; 1 Corinthians 5:6-8; Galatians 5:9). The deep cleaning of a home before Passover is a vivid reminder that we are to cleanse not just our homes but also our hearts from sin.

Each year Jewish families retell and experience anew the Exodus through the *seder* ("SAY-dur"). From the Hebrew word meaning "order," the seder is a formal festival meal that has an entirely different focus and purpose than any other meal of the year. The seder is to be held on the first night of the Passover observance. After the destruction of the Temple in AD 70, Passover became a home-centered observance.

A written order of service, called a *Haggadah* ("hah-gah-DAH," meaning "telling"), is how seder participants remember and participate in the Exodus story. All five senses are involved: There are elements to see; a story, songs, and prayers to hear; and ceremonial foods to smell, taste, and touch. Everyone from youngest to oldest is involved as the story is retold, following certain forms and including specific prayers, songs, and Scripture readings.

Within this structure, however, there has always been room for adaptation. Every person who leads a seder is free to shape the material to the needs of the group or the circumstances under which the Passover is being celebrated. For instance, Jews who are experiencing persecution have very different, secret seder experiences than those who live in relative security and peace. You can get a sense of the wide variety of interpretations of how to best recount the Passover narrative by typing "Passover Haggadah" in Amazon's search engine. When I checked recently, there were more than two thousand different options available for purchase.

During my childhood, our family used a Haggadah published by Maxwell House Coffee.[1] The iconic blue booklet, with its story of freedom for the captives, has been published by the coffee company for more than eighty years. It was available at the local supermarket in our predominately Jewish neighborhood.

SLAVES TO SIN

Passover is a celebration of God's deliverance of the Hebrew people. This deliverance should have made them free. But were they? A skim through the rest of the Old Testament, or a quick review of human history, answers that question.

Enter Jesus. More than a millennium after the Chosen People followed Moses into the desert, Jesus called the descendants of these people to repentance, telling them he'd come to save fallen humanity from our enslavement to sin (Matthew 4:17; John 3:16-18).

After his baptism, Jesus was led by the Spirit into the desert for forty days. This number, forty, and the destination, the desert, had clear symbolic meaning to the Jewish people. The Exodus story was and continues to be foundational to Jewish identity. The forty years of desert wandering prepared the Chosen People to enter the Promised Land (Numbers 32:13; Deuteronomy 29:5). This time of personal exodus following his baptism was meant to prepare Jesus for what came next. When he returned home to Nazareth, he headed to the synagogue, as was his custom on Shabbat. There the scroll was unrolled to the weekly reading from the Prophets. Jesus stood up to give voice to Isaiah 61:1-2:

> The Spirit of the Lord is on me,
>> because he has anointed me
>> to proclaim good news to the poor.
> He has sent me to proclaim freedom for the prisoners
>> and recovery of sight for the blind,
> to set the oppressed free,
>> to proclaim the year of the Lord's favor.
>
> LUKE 4:18-19

The usual pattern after a passage was read in synagogue was for the learned in the congregation to offer commentary, ask questions of the text and one another, and engage in lively debate about what the Almighty One required of them. But this day, instead of doing any of those things, Jesus closed the scroll and sat down, an act denoting authority. Instead of commentary, questions, or debate, Jesus' next words left no room for discussion: "Today this scripture is fulfilled in your hearing" (Luke 4:21).

Though at first his hearers were intrigued, they turned on him, chasing him to a cliff hugging the edge of town. In the ensuing uproar, he slipped away and began doing exactly what he'd promised to do—setting captives and oppressed people free, showing them the way to return home to God. In this, however, the Jewish Jesus was offering his followers not an escape plan from their Jewishness but a completion and deepening of it. When he delivered his Sermon on the Mount, Jesus emphasized that he'd come to fulfill the Law (Matthew 5:17). Bible teacher Lois Tverberg explains:

"Fulfill the Torah" is a rabbinic idiom that is still in use even today. The word we read as "law" is torah *in Hebrew, and its main sense is teaching, guidance and instruction, rather than legal regulation. It is God's instructions for living, and because of God's great authority, it demands obedience and therefore takes on the sense of "law." The Torah is often understood to mean the first five books of the Bible, but also refers to the Scriptures in general. In Jesus' time, and among Jews today, this is a very positive thing—that the God who made us would give us instructions for how to live. The rabbis made it their goal to understand these instructions fully and teach people how to live by it.*[2]

Tverberg notes that the Hebrew word for "to fulfill" is *lekayem* ("le-KAI-yem"), a word that signifies upholding or establishing something, as well as fulfilling, completing, or accomplishing something.[3] Every single shading of meaning of *lekayem* in Jesus' ministry can be seen in the way in which he partook of his final Passover, hours before his arrest, trial, and crucifixion. Jesus upheld the message and meaning of the seder as he applied its story of deliverance to himself.

When we read the Gospel accounts of the last meal Jesus shared with his disciples before his crucifixion (Matthew 26:17-30; Mark 14:12-26; Luke 22:7-23; John 13–17), we can see the references to the basic elements of the seder as it is still celebrated today. Jesus took these elements and adapted them to demonstrate to his disciples how he'd come to fulfill (*lekayem*) the purpose and meaning behind this yearly reenactment of God's deliverance of his people. Just as others leading seders have done before and since, Jesus reframed the traditional texts and rituals of the holiday to infuse them with new meaning.

The first hint of this came as Jesus shed his outer clothing, assumed the posture of a servant, and washed the feet of his disciples. He did so in the place of the traditional hand washing and prayer before meals, an acted entreaty for purity and a mark of willing obedience to God's commandments. Jesus underscored the foot washing with "a new command":

> Love one another. As I have loved you, so you must love one another. By this everyone will know that you are my disciples, if you love one another.   JOHN 13:34-35

The hand-washing ritual hearkened back to God's requirement that priests cleanse their hands and feet before entering the Temple to offer sacrifices (Exodus 30:17-21). Jesus' improvisation on the hand-washing ritual modeled for his disciples the humble, volitional surrender at the heart of true worship. His command to love one another flows from his sacrificial love for us. To love as he loves is made possible only by immersion in God's mercy.

After the celebratory main course of the seder, the meal continues with the final piece of unleavened bread and the third cup of wine, known in the seder as the "Cup of Redemption." Jesus infused stunning new meaning into these two essential elements of the meal, telling his disciples that these elements were about him and entreating them to continue to share them in remembrance of him (Luke 22:14-20). The Greek word used here for remembrance is *anamnēsis*, which points at the kind of active remembering that you find in muscle memory—the kind of thing that happens when you jump on a bike after not riding for years and every part of you is summoned into service as you pedal like an old pro. It is remembering by doing, not simply by thinking about a set of facts. Jesus was telling his disciples that they'd be participating with him, *anamnēsis*-style, every time they shared these elements together.

Different Christian faith traditions have different understandings of the exact nature of Communion. What I most want to emphasize here is that in light of the Passover narrative, and of Jesus' fulfillment of it, Communion is anything but a little snack.

UNLEAVENED BREAD AND FIRST FRUITS

The key symbols of Passover—a perfect lamb, slain so its blood would cover the lives of those who obeyed God's command the night of the tenth plague in Egypt, and unleavened bread, a symbol of haste in flight without the leaven of sin—unfolded with new meaning when the sinless Lamb of God was crucified. On the third day after his death, corresponding with the Feast of the First Fruits, Jesus was resurrected from the grave. Paul uses very specific language to talk with his friends about the Resurrection in Corinth:

> Christ has indeed been raised from the dead, the firstfruits
> of those who have fallen asleep. For since death came
> through a man, the resurrection of the dead comes also
> through a man. For as in Adam all die, so in Christ all
> will be made alive. But each in turn: Christ, the firstfruits;
> then, when he comes, those who belong to him.   1
>
> CORINTHIANS 15:20-23

Here it is: *lekayem.* The Passover holy days fulfilled perfectly in Jesus the Messiah.

One Jewish rabbi notes that "if Passover is largely about Egypt, Easter is largely about Passover."[4] While this may be a surprising observation from someone who does not know Jesus as Messiah, he is absolutely correct about the relationship between the two! The first time I participated in a seder at a Messianic congregation after I came to faith in Jesus, I was both stunned and overjoyed. Jesus' fingerprints were all over every movement and prayer of the ancient ritual meal—now that I'd been given eyes of faith to see them.

EVERYDAY ETERNITY: PASSOVER

The seder's foundation for the gift of Communion gives it an essential place as a teaching tool in the life of a follower of Jesus. Some Christians have made some form of a seder meal part of their Holy Week observances. Others have made it part of their family's life and worship each year. I'd like to believe that if the young girl who told me that Communion was a snack had gone to a well-presented seder led by a follower of Jesus, she probably would have understood the matzo and cup much differently.

If you're wondering how to connect more fully with these holy days that were so key in Jesus' final days on earth, I'd suggest first spending some time in Scripture. Reacquaint yourself with the Passover narrative by reading Exodus 1–15. Then see how Jesus participated in this major Jewish feast by reading Matthew 26:17-30, Mark 14:12-26, Luke 22:7-23, and John 13–17.

There are a number of excellent Passover Haggadot (plural of the singular *Haggadah*) designed specifically for Christians. They highlight ways in which Jesus fulfilled this story at each point in the seder. (See the appendix of additional resources for a few suggestions.) Participating in a seder at least once can be of great learning value for your family or small group. You'll never see Communion quite the same way again once you've experienced it in the context Jesus gave it to us.

Finally, during Passover, pray for a revelation of Jesus the Messiah for the Jewish people participating in seders around the world. The Scriptures and prayers found in most Haggadot highlight humanity's ongoing need for deliverance. May the Holy Spirit unveil hearts and lead many to freedom (2 Corinthians 3:13-18).

5

FIFTY DAYS AND FIRST FRUITS

Shavuot

IT MAY HAVE BEEN A SIMPLE, humble meal, or it might have been a banquet. Scripture doesn't list what was on the menu. But from the disciples' point of view, sharing a meal with their resurrected Lord surely made even rough bread and fish a feast.

The doubts and the jostling for position had melted away among them in the still-fresh wonder of the empty tomb. Around the table with Jesus, it must have felt like heaven on earth.

It was around one of those shared meals that Jesus told his disciples to stay together in Jerusalem. They'd soon receive a baptism of a kind they hadn't yet experienced: an immersion into the Holy Spirit.

Shortly after he gave them these instructions, Jesus returned to his Father. And the disciples waited obediently, not knowing exactly what they were waiting for. Scripture tells us, "When the day of Pentecost came, they were all together in one place" (Acts 2:1).

Modern readers may imagine that someone decided to dub

this day, when the Holy Spirit touched down like an F5 tornado, "Pentecost," a Greek-sounding word that probably meant either "tongues of fire" or "hello, Holy Spirit." The word *Pentecost* is in fact Greek in origin; it comes from the Greek word for "fifty" (*pentekostos*) and is what Greek-speaking Jews called the holiday of *Shavuot* ("Shah-voo-OT").

If we could go back in time to just a few days before the events described in Acts 2, we'd hear the resurrected Jesus telling his friends he was going to empower them to carry to the ends of the earth the news that new life was found only in him. Jesus spoke cryptically about how this empowering would happen. "I am going to send you what my Father has promised; but stay in the city until you have been clothed with power from on high" (Luke 24:49).

These Jewish followers of Jesus already knew they'd be staying in Jerusalem. From all across the land, the people who'd worshipped at the Temple in Jerusalem fifty days earlier at Passover would return for corporate worship at Shavuot, the second of the three yearly pilgrim festivals God mandated for his people.

NUMBERING THE DAYS

Shavuot, also known as the Feast of Weeks, was embedded into the rhythm of the agricultural year for the Chosen People. It provided them a way in which they could fully and faithfully respond in worship to God's provision and care for them.

To discover the way Shavuot was meant to be observed for a thousand years before Christ, you'd look back on the festal calendar to the second day of the Passover holy days, the beginning of the Feast of Unleavened Bread. The center of the celebration was the act of bringing an offering to God. Per God's instruction, each family brought to the Temple an *omer*, or about half a gallon of the just-ripened springtime barley harvest. This offering launched for the people the marking of seven weeks, or forty-nine days. On the fiftieth day, the people were called to bring another offering, this time from the "first fruit" of wheat, which was the final variety of life-giving grain to ripen during the growing season. (Scriptures detailing how the people were to observe this holiday can be found in Exodus 23:16; 34:22; Leviticus 23:15-22; Numbers 28:26-31; and Deuteronomy 16:9-12.)

This combination of offerings was a tangible way of acknowledging that God had provided everything the people needed to survive: seed, soil, and sun. He created, he provided, he sustained. As the people gathered in community to present themselves and the first and best of what God had given them, they expressed what it meant for them to be in this kind of relationship with God.

There is a beautiful contrast and symmetry in the two major Jewish springtime pilgrim festivals. Passover's story is told in part through unleavened bread, eaten in haste, in recollection of God's deliverance of the people from slavery in Egypt. Passover recounts what God had done for them. Fifty days later, Shavuot was about celebrating God's provision of the final crop of the spring. The people brought fresh, yeasty loaves and other offerings of gratitude to the Giver of these good gifts. Shavuot was the epilogue to the Exodus story—sacrifice replaced with abundance, haste replaced with celebration.

The first, best offerings of each new crop were known as the first fruits. They were a tangible expression of corporate thankfulness for the covenantal relationship with the One who'd not only delivered them from slavery but also continued to husband them at each step of their journey.

ONCE UPON A TIME IN BETHLEHEM

Traditionally on Shavuot, the book of Ruth is read. Ruth's story is a natural complement to the feast, with its themes of harvest (Ruth 2:1–3:5) and faithful response to God's covenant (Ruth 3:6–4:16).

The book of Ruth tells the story of a family driven by famine from their home in the Promised Land decades after the Hebrew people had first settled in it. The family moved from Bethlehem across the border into Moab, in what is modern-day Jordan. Naomi, the mother, married her two sons to non-Jewish local girls.

Naomi's husband and sons died while sojourning in Moab, and the bereft Naomi realized her best chance of survival would be to head home to Bethlehem. She must have been one amazing mother-in-law, because both of her newly widowed daughters-in-law, Ruth and Orpah, begged to leave their own hometown in order to accompany her back to Bethlehem. Mama Naomi was able to convince Orpah to return to her parents' home, but Ruth refused to be pried from Naomi's side.

The two women came to Bethlehem and found provision there as Ruth went to work. She gleaned the grain intentionally left behind in the fields of Boaz, a relative of Naomi's deceased husband. God had mandated this practice in Leviticus 19:9-10 and 23:22 as a just way to ensure that even the poorest members of the community had a way to provide for themselves and their families. Boaz noticed the way in which the young, foreign woman cared so tenderly for her mother-in-law. And Naomi noticed Boaz's God-fearing character and believed this man would do the right thing for her and her beloved Ruth. He indeed did, acting as an agent of God's redeeming love and enfolding this foreign-born girl into the goodness of God's covenant relationship with his people during a remarkable exchange that took place in the midst of the grain harvest season.

Ruth's marriage to Boaz was a fruitful one. The Bible tells us she was King David's great-grandmother (Ruth 4:17) and became a part of the royal line leading through time all the way to Jesus' birth in Bethlehem (Matthew 1:5).

FROM SHEAVES TO TABLETS

The Jerusalem Temple was destroyed in AD 70. To maintain their unique identity, the Jewish people needed to reframe the Temple-centered faith of their ancestors. Prayer and works of charity replaced the sacrificial system, and the cycle of holy days became untethered from the land-based agricultural rhythms of the Jewish people. Many of them were persecuted and forcibly dispersed from their homeland. Some became slaves, and others eventually fathered communities in far-flung cities and towns. Jewish practice needed to be portable, which meant focusing on the embedded spiritual message within each of their feasts.

Shavuot shifted quite dramatically in meaning and practice during this period. Instead of a holiday celebrating the wheat harvest and God's provision, Shavuot became identified with the giving of the Law to the Israelites at Mount Sinai. This was not a random reassignment, however; the learned scholars did some calculating based on a clue found in Exodus 19:1:

On the first day of the third month after the Israelites left Egypt—on that very day—they came to the Desert of Sinai.

These Torah scholars eventually determined that the Israelites received the Ten Commandments fifty days after their departure from Egypt.

God's gift of the Law became the focus of a Shavuot celebration, in the absence of a Temple where the people could bring their agricultural offerings. Because the word *Shavuot* is related to the Hebrew word for "oath," some Jewish sages have likened the act of God giving the Law to the Chosen People at Sinai to a wedding sealing the covenant between God and his people.

ALL-NIGHTERS AND CHEESECAKE

Shavuot is generally not observed at the same level (if at all) as Passover, Rosh Hashanah/Yom Kippur, or Chanukah. Some have suggested that this holiday's lack of shared ritual meals (like the seder) or recognizable symbols (like the menorah) have kept this day from catching on with all but the most observant members of the Jewish community. Within that group, Shavuot is celebrated today by spending some or all of the night awake in Bible study and prayer.

Dairy foods (cheesecake!) are a food tradition on Shavuot. Some rabbis have suggested that when the Chosen People received the kosher laws (detailed in Deuteronomy 11:1-47; 14:3-20) as part of the larger Torah given at Sinai, they realized that their cooking utensils were not set up to cook meat and dairy dishes separately; the Hebrew people ate uncooked dairy dishes in response to this law (Exodus 23:19; 24:26; Deuteronomy 14:21). Others have suggested that eating dairy with honey is a way to honor the language of the Torah as being sweet, rich, and fulfilling, just as milk and honey are to us (Song of Songs 4:11). Still others have noted that the custom may simply derive from Shavuot's roots in the agricultural cycle: In antiquity, cheese was often made in late spring.

Shavuot is a holy day laden with significance for followers of Jesus. We'll be looking in depth at how the Christian calendar marks Pentecost in chapter seventeen, but in this space we'll reflect on the meaning of the holiday Jesus observed during his lifetime, as well as what the postbiblical practice of the holiday can teach us about how to celebrate the incredible gift of God's Word to us.

EVERYDAY ETERNITY: SHAVUOT

The Bible is so accessible to us that it's easy to take it for granted. We find inspirational Bible verses printed on mugs, notepads, and other *tchotchkes* ("CHOCH-kas" or "CHOCH-keys," a Yiddish word for trinkets or dust-collecting bits of household clutter). We have the Bible available to us in dozens of versions—in print, on websites, and via apps. There are hundreds of thousands of resources available to us to interpret and apply the riches of the Word of God: commentaries, books, conferences, sermons, seminars, broadcasts, and podcasts. Yet with this vast library of teaching at our fingertips, our culture is marked by a growing apathy toward the Bible. According to a 2014 survey commissioned by the American Bible Society, 88 percent of households in this country own at least one Bible, but only 37 percent of us reported reading it once a week or more, and 26 percent of American adults never read the Bible.[1]

Whether we cherish God's Word or take it for granted, Shavuot can be for us an opportunity to renew our relationship with the Bible. While there are always some of us who begin each new calendar year with grand plans to read the Bible through in a year, or memorize this passage or that one, the joy of Shavuot is in responding to God's revelation of himself to humanity through his Word. Rather than an arbitrary starting point such as January 1, our covenant history with God can be the place from which we consider how to more deeply engage with Scripture each year.

When he gave Moses the Ten Commandments at Mount Sinai, God was forming these former slaves into a people who would learn to reflect his character to the nations around them. God had always initiated a relationship with the people he created, and when he gave his people the written Law, he told them precisely how they were to live in right relationship with him and with one another.

Implicit in the Mosaic covenant established at Sinai is an incredible promise:

"The days are coming," declares the LORD,
 "when I will make a new covenant
with the people of Israel
 and with the people of Judah.
It will not be like the covenant
 I made with their ancestors
when I took them by the hand
 to lead them out of Egypt,
because they broke my covenant,
 though I was a husband to them,"
            declares the LORD.
"This is the covenant I will make with the people of Israel
 after that time," declares the LORD.
"I will put my law in their minds
 and write it on their hearts.
I will be their God,
 and they will be my people.
No longer will they teach their neighbor,

or say to one another, 'Know the LORD,'
because they will all know me,
from the least of them to the greatest,"

declares the LORD.

"For I will forgive their wickedness
and will remember their sins no more."

JEREMIAH 31:31-34

This promise would take on new meaning to the Jewish followers of Jesus on the very first Shavuot after Jesus' death, resurrection, and ascension, with the coming of the Holy Spirit, which we commemorate today on the day of *Pentecost*.

Some of us battle with guilt about our level of engagement with Scripture. Some may have a sense of disconnection with it because of painful losses or negative experiences with other believers. There is ample space in this life to wrestle with what the Bible says, to ask questions of the text, to seek understanding. Those struggles are in fact part of the gift of Shavuot. That they exist affirms that the Bible is not like any other book on the planet.

Shavuot is not a memorial of a once-upon-a-time event that happened to someone else but an ongoing conversation with the Author and finisher of our faith. The story of Ruth, read on Shavuot, is a beautiful reminder that God invites us into a covenant with him.

On Shavuot, you, your family, and your church can stop and savor the sweetness of God's Word. Read Exodus 19:1–20:21, which details God giving the Ten Commandments to Moses, to be given to his people. Meditate on what this passage tells you about the character of God. What is he asking of you in response?

Consider reading aloud the book of Ruth in a Bible version or paraphrase different from the one you normally use. What do you notice about the story as a result?

Instead of the New Year's resolutions you've made in the past to read the Bible every day, or in a year, or to simply dig in more deeply, why not quietly take one of those steps at this time of year?

Finally, in honor of Shavuot, why not enjoy a dairy feast—or maybe just a slice of cheesecake?

6

MAY YOU BE INSCRIBED
IN THE BOOK OF LIFE

Rosh Hashanah, Feast of Trumpets

FOR MANY OF US, September has the feeling of a new year. It's back-to-school time. The meandering of August gives way to a quicker cadence after Labor Day.

For Jewish people observing the festal cycle, September *is* the new year. Rosh Hashanah ("ROESH ha-shah-NAH"), meaning "head of the year," launches the beginning of the fall cycle of feasts. This can be a bit confusing, as the spring month of Nisan is counted as the first month of the Jewish calendar. Nisan is when the first religious feast of the year, Passover, is celebrated. The Jewish *civil* year, however, begins with Rosh Hashanah. Jewish years are numbered from Rosh Hashanah; one Jewish year gives way to the next on Rosh Hashanah in the same way that January 1 begins a new year on the Gregorian calendar. God gave the fall feasts—Rosh Hashanah, Yom Kippur (Day of Atonement), and Sukkot (Feast of Tabernacles)—in order to help his people consider their origins, reflect on who they are in the present, and prepare for their spiritual future.

The first of this triad of fall festivals, Rosh Hashanah, is also known as the Feast of Trumpets. It is described in Leviticus 23:23-25:

> The LORD said to Moses, "Say to the Israelites: 'On the first day of the seventh month you are to have a day of sabbath rest, a sacred assembly commemorated with trumpet blasts. Do no regular work, but present a food offering to the LORD.'"

From this spare pair of sentences given to the Chosen People in the desert, Rosh Hashanah has taken on additional layers of meaning. The Feast of Trumpets launches a ten-day period of deep self-examination known as the Days of Awe. They serve as preparation for Yom Kippur, the most solemn day of the entire Jewish year. In a similar way that Christmas and Easter services increase church attendance beyond regular weekly services, many Jewish people who aren't regular synagogue attenders will find their way to High Holiday services at Rosh Hashanah and Yom Kippur. Others in the Jewish community who don't attend services will still gather with family and friends for a traditional holiday feast. Even when other ritual practices fall away, tradition—in the form of food—continues to connect families to their history and identity.

At Rosh Hashanah, the big family meal includes sweet foods such as apples, dates, honey, and a round loaf of challah ("cHAH-luh"), a moist, egg-rich yeast bread. It's an edible wish for a sweet new year. The traditional Rosh Hashanah greeting points toward the deeper meaning of the holy day: *L'shanah tovah tikkatevu* ("Lah-shah-NAH toe-VAH teek-ah-TAY-voo"), or its shorter form, *L'shanah tovah* ("Lah-shah-NAH toe-VAH"), meaning "May you be inscribed for a good year."

Inscribed where? In God's Book of Life. The phrase "Book of Life" is mentioned in conjunction with God's judgment in both the Old Testament (Exodus 32:31-32; Psalm 69:28; 139:16; Malachi 3:16-18) and the New (Philippians 4:3 and throughout the book of Revelation).

Rosh Hashanah's feasting and sweet treats heighten the importance of this holiday. Rosh Hashanah is first and foremost a call to repentance and spiritual preparation. It has also come to be known in the Jewish community as the anniversary of God's creation of humankind, the day in which God said, "Let us make mankind in our image" (Genesis 1:26). Rabbis and sages long, long ago used Scripture's time markers to calculate that Rosh Hashanah was indeed humanity's birth date.

Writer Paul Steinberg described the dual themes of repentance and creation of this holiday:

> *Though it is a day to rewind time, by its end we are to be inspired to look forward and "sing to the LORD a new song" (Ps. 96:1). After all, remembering is the primary Jewish action—we are never to forget. Remembering and hearkening back to our beginnings reinvigorates us with a new life, a new time, a new song.*[1]

WAKE UP!

The holy day of Rosh Hashanah carries with it a built-in siren designed to rouse the people into spiritual readiness. The shofar was used in a variety of different formats. Made of a ram's horn, it was a primitive trumpet used to rally troops for battle. It was also used to mark the beginning of a new month, to alert the people when an enemy was attacking, and to announce the coronation of a new king. When the walls of Jericho fell, it was to the sound of shofar blasts (Joshua 6:4-20). The instrument was also used in Temple worship (Psalm 150:5). The sound is not like any other sound on earth. Every time I've heard its blast, I feel its imperatives in the very marrow of my bones: *Wake up! The time to act is now!*

Though Rosh Hashanah has come to include the celebration of God's creation of humankind, the creation account is not the focus of holiday readings at synagogues the world over. Instead, for generations the key readings have been the biblical accounts of the birth of Isaac and the binding of this long-awaited son of Abraham on Mount Moriah. Found in Genesis 21–22, it is the story of a fully awake and completely obedient Abraham. The urgency of obedience and the faith to act flies in the face of purely human reasoning. The story itself is a shofar blast.

At age seventy-five, Abram had obeyed God's call to leave his home in Ur (modern-day Iraq) and follow him into the unknown. God initiated a covenant with this barren septuagenarian, promising to make him the father of a great nation (Genesis 12:2). When Abram was ninety-nine, God again visited him, giving new names to him and his antique, barren wife, Sarai: Abram became Abraham ("father of many"); Sarai became Sarah ("princess"). These new names were a sign of a new identity given by God to the elderly pair.

To mark the covenant God initiated with Abraham, God required that all the males in Abraham's family undergo circumcision (Genesis 17:11-14). This distinctive physical marker would be a daily, intimate reminder of God's covenant with Abraham and his kin.

The nonagenarian Abraham obeyed God, and a year later,

improbably and miraculously, he and Sarah became the parents of Isaac.

Fast-forward another thirteen years, and we arrive at the story that shapes Rosh Hashanah observance. Isaac is a young man when God tells Abraham to bring his son to the land of Moriah and offer up his son on the mountain to which he'll direct the pair. Abraham and Isaac travel three days to the top of Mount Moriah, the eventual site of Solomon's Temple. (It now houses Islam's third-holiest site, the Dome of the Rock.) They carry firewood with them to offer the sacrifice to God, and the innocent young man asks his father where the lamb for their offering is. Abraham responds, "God himself will provide the lamb for the burnt offering" (Genesis 22:8).

At the top of the low mountain, Abraham asks his son to trust him. He binds the young man—this impossible, beautiful, miraculous boy—to a heap of stacked wood. Abraham pulls his knife from its sheath and readies himself to slit his beloved son's throat in order to obey his Lord's command.

What must it have been like to look into the eyes of this miracle boy and be faced with the impossible choice: either God or his son? How long did Abraham wrestle in silent prayer before he slowly raised his knife-clenched hand in the air?

God stops Abraham in the nick of time. In the span of a single heartbeat, Abraham spots a perfect ram to offer God, tangled by its horn in a nearby bramble. Abraham names the sacred spot *Jehovah Jireh*, which means "the LORD will provide."

The moment when Abraham enacted his "Yes, Lord" was eternal in nature. We still reflect on his choice, and we still benefit from his willingness to obey even when it would have cost him his own beloved child. God blessed the old man for his unflinching obedience and again repeated the promise of a homeland and descendants too numerous to count, through whom God would bless the entire earth (Genesis 22:15-18). At Rosh Hashanah, the shofar is a link across time to God's provision of the ram. Abraham's single-minded trust is a tutor for generations of descendants, who are meant to hear in the piercing blast of the shofar a call to live in a way worthy of having their names inscribed in the Book of Life.

REPENT AND RETURN

Abraham's story may provide important commentary about the seriousness with which God takes his covenant, but it is the sound of the shofar that applies the message of that story to those who hear its eerie, piercing blasts. Rosh Hashanah's association as the birthday of humankind adds another layer of meaning to the shofar's call. As there was a beginning of time in creation, there will be an end of days. Rosh Hashanah's message of repentance points to the Creator as the only one who has the right to judge the acts and intentions of those he created. He is the only one who can inscribe or delete our names from his Book of Life.

The shofar is a summons for each individual to make an unflinching inventory of his or her life, acknowledge wrongdoing, confess sin to God (and others who have been hurt by a sinful action), and live in a different way that honors God. Rosh Hashanah initiates this period of repentance in preparation for the coming day of judgment.

Perhaps the most poignant picture of the Feast of Trumpets in the Old Testament is found in Nehemiah 7:73–8:18, which describes the first time the Feast of Trumpets was celebrated after the return from Babylonian captivity. After seventy years, some of the Jewish people had been miraculously permitted to return to their land. There was no welcome-home party in Jerusalem for these exiles. The city had been sacked, then left in disrepair for seven decades. Though a few hardy souls who hadn't been deported had lingered in or near the city, Jerusalem was in ruins.

The groups who returned to the city rebuilt the Temple and city walls. Those who oversaw the building were concerned about far more than a successful reconstruction project, however. They wanted to see a spiritual renovation take place among the people of Jerusalem. The people convened for Rosh Hashanah as the Torah commanded, on the first day of the seventh month. They asked Ezra, one of their spiritual leaders, to read aloud to them from the Law.

Ezra read from daybreak until midday. The Word pierced the souls of the gathered crowd like a shofar sounding an alarm. Their dawning understanding became deep conviction as the morning continued. Sorrow became open weeping. They'd returned physically, but they realized they were still far from the One who'd brought them there. Those tears of repentance moved them from the survival-level faith they'd maintained during their enslavement in Babylon to the freedom of serving God in Jerusalem.

The leaders recognized the joy buried in the repentant sorrow of the people. Nehemiah comforted the overwrought people with these instructions: "Go and enjoy choice food and sweet drinks, and send some to those who have nothing prepared. This day is holy to our Lord. Do not grieve, for the joy of the Lord is your strength" (Nehemiah 8:10).

His words continue to define the way in which the message of repentance at Rosh Hashanah is observed. Repentance leads us to restoration. The shofar blast gives way to sweet treats.

THE KINGDOM OF GOD IS AT HAND

More than four hundred years after Ezra read the Law to the Jewish people in Jerusalem, a largely Jewish audience flooded into the desert to hear John the Baptist trumpet a single message: Repent, because the kingdom of God is on the scene (Mark 1:4). John's one-note pronouncement to the people—that they were to change heart, mind, and direction in order to return to God—was familiar language for this crowd. When John told his hearers that the Kingdom of God was at hand, they understood the words as referring to the coming day of final judgment of the world by the wholly righteous Creator and Ruler. John's Jewish audience knew the end of days was when the long-awaited Messiah would restore the world to its created order.

John directed his audiences toward Jesus. And during his ministry, Jesus directed his own audiences to the end of days:

As lightning that comes from the east is visible even in the west, so will be the coming of the Son of Man. Wherever there is a carcass, there the vultures will gather.
Immediately after the distress of those days

"the sun will be darkened,
and the moon will not give its light;
the stars will fall from the sky,
and the heavenly bodies will be shaken."

Then will appear the sign of the Son of Man in heaven. And then all the peoples of the earth will mourn when they see the Son of Man coming on the clouds of heaven, with power and great glory. And he will send his angels with a loud trumpet call, and they will gather his elect from the four winds, from one end of the heavens to the other. MATTHEW 24:27-31

The Greek word Jesus used to describe the coming of the Son in this passage, *parousia* ("pah-ROO-zee-uh"), denoted the arrival of an important visitor. It is used a number of times throughout the New Testament in reference to the second coming of Christ.[2] When a king or dignitary approached a city, the people would already be watching and waiting anxiously for him. They'd head out to provide a royal welcome to the honored guest before he arrived at the city gates. You can see the way in which *parousia* worked in Jesus' day in the parable of the five foolish and five wise virgins found in Matthew 25:1-13. The young women were tasked with watching for the bridegroom, then going out to greet him in order to accompany him back to the wedding feast: "At midnight the cry rang out: 'Here's the bridegroom! Come out to meet him!'" (verse 6). The five who were prepared with oil lamps left their waiting spot and ran to greet him. The five who were unprepared had to go instead on a midnight search for lamp oil. Those unfortunate young ladies lost their opportunity to celebrate the arrival of the bridegroom and were shut out of the wedding.

As followers of Jesus, we've been given ears to hear the message of the shofar's piercing wake-up call. May we live our lives in readiness every day of the year so we can welcome with awe and joy the returning King to the world he made.

EVERYDAY ETERNITY: ROSH HASHANAH

Followers of Jesus can embrace Rosh Hashanah's emphasis on creation, the end of days, and our need to live in readiness through repentance. Scripture readings that may enhance your reflection on these themes include Genesis 1–2, Psalm 51, Psalm 103, Matthew 24–25, and Revelation 21–22.

There is a lovely ceremony on the afternoon of Rosh Hashanah that captures the essence of what it means to respond to the call to return to right relationship with the covenant-making, covenant-keeping God. The ritual is called *Tashlich* ("tash-LEEKH"), or "casting off." Micah 7:18-19 forms the foundation of Tashlich:

> Who is a God like you,
>> who pardons sin and forgives the transgression
>> of the remnant of his inheritance?
>
> You do not stay angry forever
>> but delight to show mercy.
>
> You will again have compassion on us;
>> you will tread our sins underfoot
>> and hurl all our iniquities into the depths of the sea.

Individuals or groups arrive at a stream or river with pieces of bread in hand. As prayers are recited, each person quietly names his or her specific sin against God and tosses the bread into the flowing water. Every crumb is carried away. It's a poignant expression of longing for a fresh beginning with the Lord. Tashlich is a memorable way in which we can enact our prayers for repentance. Enjoying a sweet treat of apples and honey afterward can underscore the sweetness of responding to the call to return wholeheartedly to God.

If we're listening, if we're preparing our hearts, then the shofar blast will sound to us like the good news that it is: *Wake up! Your king is coming!*

7

ATONEMENT AND MERCY

Yom Kippur

WHEN I WAS A GIRL, my family occasionally attended services for Yom Kippur ("YOHM ke-PUHR"), or Day of Atonement. Many synagogues, including the one to which we belonged, sell tickets for seats at these services. This practice may sound strange to Christian ears, but because even those who don't attend synagogue regularly feel an obligation to attend these most important corporate worship services of the entire year, many synagogues use the occasion as a fundraiser for the congregation and to get a sense of how many people will be in attendance.

My family couldn't always afford to attend these services, but in our majority-Jewish neighborhood on this holiest day of the year, the schools were always closed. So even if we weren't in synagogue, we stayed bunkered inside our home until late afternoon. No one played outside on Yom Kippur.

Scripture mandates Yom Kippur as a day of fasting, but most children under age thirteen, the elderly, and those with medical conditions opt for a modified fast. I remember wondering what it was like to go without food all day, all while praying those long, aching prayers I heard the grown-ups chanting in synagogue. I remember a deep sense of unease on Yom Kippur each year. Had I repented enough and done enough good deeds to merit God's gracious inscription in his Book of Life?

Beyond my own spotty synagogue attendance, my understanding about Yom Kippur was formed by Sydney Taylor's 1954 children's book, *More All-of-a-Kind Family*. Part of a series describing the daily lives of a Jewish immigrant family at the turn of the twentieth century, its chapter about the holy day helped me imagine what Yom Kippur might have been like when my grandparents were young. The story recounts Yom Kippur from the children's perspective, beginning with the giant feast the family shared before sundown in order to sustain them through a long day of fasting. At one point in the chapter, the children purchase some flowers from a Gentile shopkeeper to bring to their mother in the synagogue, in hopes of making her fast day a little easier. This Yom Kippur fast was serious, challenging business.

Taylor's explanation of what Yom Kippur must have been like when the Temple was still standing in Jerusalem painted for me an unforgettable portrait of God's holiness. After describing the days of physical and spiritual preparation undertaken by the high priest, she describes the central event of Yom Kippur:

> *Amidst all the splendor in the Temple at Jerusalem, there was one small chamber which boasted no wonderful golden objects, no luxurious hangings. It was considered the Holy of Holies, because it was the place where the spirit of God was thought to rest. The curtains to this room always remained*

closed. They opened for but one man—the High Priest; for but one day—Yom Kippur. . . .

He donned a simple white linen gown. He chanted a prayer confessing his sins and the sins of all, and, holding a vessel of burning incense in his hands, he entered the Holy of Holies. The curtains closed behind him.

No one knew what went on in the small chamber, but in the Temple courtyards the priests and, behind them, the congregation of men and women, anxiously watched the circles of smoke rise through the folds of the curtain— watched and prayed.

When the High Priest emerged at last, shouts of joy burst from the lips of the people.[1]

Though Taylor didn't come out and say it, her description of the people's anxiety as they watched and prayed underscored what I knew from my own Yom Kippur synagogue attendance. This day was about life and death. There was no middle ground on Yom Kippur.

Today, nearly two thousand years after the destruction of the Temple in Jerusalem, the long, long day of prayer in synagogues around the world still captures the deep longing of the Jewish people to be found acceptable in the sight of a perfectly holy, completely righteous God.

YOM KIPPUR IN THE BIBLE

When Adam and Eve were banished from the Garden of Eden, God sealed the entrance to this perfect space with a physical barrier that prevented their return. In spelling out the consequences for their sin, God embedded a promise that he himself would vanquish sin and restore humanity to full fellowship with him (Genesis 3:15). In the meantime, however, there remained that wall of separation. When God gave Moses the Law, he showed the people created in his image what holiness was like by detailing what was and wasn't acceptable in his sight. In the description of the Tabernacle and the Temple that followed, God tasked his people with creating a house of prayer for all nations. This was a key way in which they'd fulfill their light-bearing role to the world, inviting all to draw near to God. Yet in the physical structures God commanded them to construct, there was always a reminder of the separation between them, a thick veil that kept them from entering the Holy of Holies.

The sacrificial offerings detailed in the book of Leviticus gave the Hebrew people a way to worship God and to restore their relationship with him. Most of us in Western society are disconnected from animal slaughter, so we may not know what to do with the lengthy descriptions in the Law about ritual sacrifice. Yet the words of Leviticus 17:11 tell us something we sense as truly as we know our own heartbeat: "The life of a creature is in the blood, and I have given it to you to make atonement for yourselves on the altar; it is the blood that makes atonement for one's life." Atonement is doing what is needed to repair a wrong we've done. It takes life to make atonement for sin before God, the holy Giver of life, and restore unbroken fellowship with him.

Though animal sacrifice took place all year, God prescribed one day during the year in which the high priest would enter the otherwise off-limits Holy of Holies to meet with God in order to intercede for his people so they could experience "at-one-ment," or restored fellowship with God. The people fasted and prayed, and the high priest prepared to intercede for the entire nation.[2]

Each year on Yom Kippur, the high priest would undergo

intense preparation, offer sacrifices to God on his own behalf and on behalf of the people, and cast lots to select one spotless male goat, over which the priest would pronounce the sins of the people. The goat was then released into the wilderness to carry the people's sins far away from the gathered community. The term *scapegoat* comes from this practice.

The high priest would then slip through the thick curtains at the entrance to the Holy of Holies, bearing coals from the sacrificial altar, along with incense, which represented the prayers of the people. He'd burn the incense so that the smoke obscured his view of the altar in the sacred space, which housed manna from the Exodus, the stone tablets with the Ten Commandments, and Aaron's staff that had miraculously produced almonds. These physical tokens of the covenant God had made with his people stood as indictments against the people who'd violated the covenant relationship. The otherwise-empty space contained the very glory of God.

The high priest sprinkled the blood of the animals he'd slain on the top of the altar in the Holy of Holies, known as the mercy seat. As he did, he made atonement for the people. Their sin was once again covered.

Yom Kippur was meant to be a day of great mercy for the people. Yet even this Day of Atonement could showcase the people's disconnection from God. Isaiah 58 contains God's indictment of his people for fasting with legalistic precision, yet missing the point of God's amazing grace toward them:

> Yet on the day of your fasting, you do as you please
>   and exploit all your workers.
> Your fasting ends in quarreling and strife,
>   and in striking each other with wicked fists.

You cannot fast as you do today
and expect your voice to be heard on high.
Is this the kind of fast I have chosen,
only a day for people to humble themselves?
Is it only for bowing one's head like a reed
and for lying in sackcloth and ashes?
Is that what you call a fast,
a day acceptable to the LORD?

ISAIAH 58:3-5

Yom Kippur was a mercy from God, meant to move God's people to reflect his just, loving character by their actions: feeding the hungry, clothing the naked, sheltering the poor, caring well for one's family members, and setting captives free (Isaiah 58:6-8). Seven centuries later these words would go on to characterize the ministry of Jesus.

YOM KIPPUR IN THE JEWISH COMMUNITY

After the destruction of the Temple in Jerusalem in AD 70, there was no Holy of Holies to serve as the focal point for Yom Kippur. Synagogue-based prayer services reshaped Yom Kippur observance for the Jewish community.

As with all other Jewish holy days, Yom Kippur begins at sunset. The evening services include the ancient *Kol Nidre* ("all vows"), a prayer in Aramaic allowing worshippers to clean their spiritual slates by renouncing past vows. Some Jewish communities include a prayer for renunciation of future vows as well. This slate-cleaning exercise is a reminder that our covenant-making, promise-keeping God takes our vows very seriously—more seriously, perhaps, than we do.

The sung or chanted *Kol Nidre* likely came into wide usage during the medieval period, when many Jews were forced to convert to Christianity or be killed. Those who gathered during those years to observe the Jewish holy days in secret would begin by renouncing the vows they'd been forced to make. A moving corporate confession of sin is a part of the evening service as well.

The next morning, worshippers say prayers in memory of family members who have passed away. Congregational leaders read aloud Scripture passages about what the Day of Atonement was like when the Temple was standing. The focus of the afternoon prayer service is the reading of the book of Jonah. The story of the reluctant prophet is read on Yom Kippur to remind worshippers that no one is beyond God's reach or above his judgment and that God responds to repentance with perfect mercy.

Linking each of these ancient prayer services is the longing for the participants' names to be inscribed in the Book of Life for the coming year. Because Yom Kippur is an annual observance, the prayer to be inscribed is an annual one as well. The last service of the day is *Neilah* ("closing the gate"), a final opportunity to seek God's forgiveness and blessing before the Book of Life is closed for the upcoming year. The shofar is blown at sunset; then families gather to share a light dairy-based meal to break the fast. This is a practical matter: Dairy meals tend to be quick and easy to prepare, and the lighter fare is easy for empty stomachs to digest.

YOM KIPPUR AND JESUS

Christians believe Jesus completely, fully cleansed us once and for all from our state of sinfulness before God.[3] Where Yom Kippur offered the Hebrew people the opportunity for cleansing that was more like spot-treating spills on a garment, Jesus' atonement offers those who trust him with their lives a complete change of status. Through Christ, God did for us what we could not do for ourselves.

Jesus demonstrated God's mercy throughout his ministry. One especially vivid example of this happened when a woman was caught in an act of adultery (John 8:1-11). There seemed to be no question of her guilt, nor the death by stoning prescribed in the Law for both the woman and her lover (Leviticus 20:10; Deuteronomy 22:22-24). Yet religious leaders dragged only the woman into a courtyard area of the Temple with the twin goals of toppling Jesus' popularity and acting as God's self-appointed judges, jury, and executioners.

The intense exchange Jesus had with these leaders culminated in his piercing response to them: "Let any one of you who is without sin be the first to throw a stone at her" (John 8:7). One by one, the stones in the leaders' hands fell to the ground. One by one, each leader walked away from the scene. Every single one of them had sinned. They were within footsteps of the Temple, the very place where they brought their own sacrifices as a confession of their sin. They were as guilty of sin as the woman shivering in terror before them.

The mercy Jesus expressed to her required her to change direction in her life: "Go now and leave your life of sin" (John 8:11). The forgiveness he extended to her, and to the marginalized, the sick, and the oppressed throughout his ministry, was Isaiah 58 in action.

The permanent change of status Jesus offers through his forgiveness was underscored during his crucifixion: "At that moment [as Jesus gave up his spirit] the curtain of the temple was torn in two from top to bottom" (Matthew 27:50-51). The curtain to which this verse refers is the heavy divider that separated the Holy of Holies from the rest of the Temple. Historian Alfred Edersheim concluded that, given the size and heft of the curtain, its top-to-bottom tearing could be nothing short of miraculous: "If the Veil was at all such as is described in the Talmud, it could not have been rent in twain by a mere earthquake or the fall of the lintel."[4] In Jesus, Yom Kippur's yearly atonement was fulfilled once and for all.

WHY PASSOVER?

Some have wondered why, if Jesus' life was a perfect sacrifice, Jesus didn't die on Yom Kippur instead of Passover. During the first decades after the Resurrection, when the early Christian community was primarily Jewish, believers continued to participate in Yom Kippur and the rest of the yearly festival cycle, though their understanding of those rituals took on new meaning as they reveled in the fulfillment of Jesus' sacrifice for them. Many of the church's early leaders taught about Jesus as simultaneously High Priest, scapegoat, and perfect sacrifice. The source material for this teaching tended to be the events of Holy Week.

But while early church leaders continued to teach Jesus' fulfillment of Yom Kippur's purpose, there was a movement among Gentile believers away from adapting Yom Kippur as a holy day for the church. Scholar Daniel Stökl Ben Ezra wrote,

> *Yom Kippur was for Gentile Christians not so much a custom to be continued as a festival to be newly adopted—a process possible only where the new custom could be supported by a Christian rationale. Since Christ died in Nisan [during Passover] and not in Tishri [during Yom Kippur], the main meaningful events of earliest Christianity were connected to a different month.*[5]

In any case, while Yom Kippur is a central event in the Jewish calendar, the Exodus is the essential narrative of the Jewish people.

Jesus' perfect sacrifice at Passover fulfilled the once-a-year reckoning of sin at Yom Kippur and atoned for the sin that is at work daily in each of our lives.

EVERYDAY ETERNITY: YOM KIPPUR

Does Yom Kippur have meaning for those seeking to follow Jesus today? Yes. Yom Kippur allows us to reflect on the immeasurable grace of God found in our Messiah Jesus. Instead of apprehension about whether we'll be inscribed in the Book of Life from year to year, Jesus' followers can embrace his fulfillment of this day with deep gratitude.

Many Messianic Jews choose to fast on Yom Kippur as a way to both stand in solidarity with and intercede in prayer for their not-yet-believing Jewish friends and family. Followers of Jesus understand that fasting is not a transaction that demonstrates how serious a person is about repenting from sin; fasting is a spiritual discipline that allows us to focus our desires on God.

If you'd like to consider the meaning of Yom Kippur more fully, consider prayerfully reflecting on the words of Isaiah 58. How did Jesus' life and ministry reflect this kind of fast? What kind of fast might God be calling you to do?

You may wish to seek out some hymns or worship songs that focus on the atonement. "There Is a Redeemer" (Melody Green), "And Can It Be?" (Wesley/Campbell), and "O Sacred Head, Now Wounded" (Bernard of Clairvaux) can get you started.

If you gather with others on Yom Kippur, thank God together for the once-and-for-all salvation he's given you in Jesus the Messiah. He has inscribed your name on the palms of his hands (Isaiah 49:16) and written it in his Book of Life (Revelation 21:27).

8

GOD WITH US, US WITH GOD

Sukkot / Feast of Tabernacles

AS SOON AS THE FASTING HUNGER PANGS of Yom Kippur fade, the attention of observant Jewish families turns to the next biblical festival of the yearly cycle: the Feast of Tabernacles.

In neighborhoods with observant Jewish populations, the days immediately following Yom Kippur are filled with activity as families erect small booth-like structures in their yards, on their balconies, or in any outdoor space they may have available. They do this in preparation for a festival that begins five days after Yom Kippur. These structures may be as simple as a few pieces of plywood and tarp hammered together, or they may be elaborate prefab structures costing several hundred dollars. The roofs are created from branches or other natural material. They must allow those inside a view of the early autumn night sky. Crayoned children's artwork, garlands, and harvest fruit and flowers decorate the temporary space.

Most synagogues erect a booth, or *sukkah* ("soo-KAH"; *sukkot* is the plural form), for community use. Those who don't have space or funds to build their own sukkah can fellowship in the communal sukkah. These temporary structures aren't meant to provide permanent shelter to anyone.

Five evenings after Yom Kippur ends, families and congregations come together for casual times of outdoor feasting and fellowship in their sukkot. The party continues for the next eight nights. Some families choose to sleep in their little booths.

Sukkot, or the Feast of Tabernacles, is the final feast of the yearly festal cycle. It is one of three pilgrim feasts (along with Passover and Shavuot) in which God called the people to leave their homes, fields, and workplaces in order to assemble together before him each year. The sukkah is the central motif of this feast:

> Live in temporary shelters for seven days: All native-born
> Israelites are to live in such shelters so your descendants
> will know that I had the Israelites live in temporary
> shelters when I brought them out of Egypt. I am the
> LORD your God. LEVITICUS 23:42-43

The experience of living in booths, even if only for a meal or two during Sukkot, underscores the pilgrim status of the Chosen People. But Sukkot is far more than a living history lesson. The immersive experience of this feast anchors participants to their identity as Exodus people delivered by God, while simultaneously pointing them toward an incredible future fulfillment of God's redemption story.

GIVE ME SHELTER

Author Michael Strassfeld suggests that the sukkah is a reminder that our safety and security comes from relationship with God:

"The sukkah makes us realize what sheltering is all about. . . . We must learn not to trust in the size or strength of our homes, nor in how filled they are with precious things. These are as broken reeds that can be swept away in a moment of ill fortune."[1]

The Feast of Tabernacles commemorates the construction of God's own sukkah, the Tabernacle (*mishkan*) he directed his people to build in the desert shortly after he delivered them from slavery in Egypt. The mishkan was designed by God to be impermanent and portable as it traveled with the Chosen People through forty years of desert sojourn and their first years in the Promised Land. The focal point of their community, the mishkan was a place of divine hospitality. It was where the glory of God dwelled and where his people could meet with him and one another.

As with the other feasts described in Leviticus 23, Sukkot is tied to the rhythms of agriculture. God directed the people to take branches from "luxuriant trees" (Leviticus 23:40) on the first day of the holiday and rejoice before God with them. Sages determined that there were four species representing the gift of the bounty God provided for them from the land: a lemon-like citrus fruit known as an etrog, the date palm tree, the myrtle bush, and the willow.[2] The date palm, myrtle, and willow branches are bound together in a large bunch called a lulav. Worshippers chant the Hallel Psalms (Psalms 113–118) while waving the bundled lulav along with the etrog to the north, south, east, and west, toward the heavens and down toward the ground. This would ensure they'd obey God's command to rejoice before him during this holiday.

More than any other Jewish holiday, Sukkot carries with it the promise of a future Messianic fulfillment. For generations, worshippers read key Scripture passages pointing toward this promise, including the description of God's glory filling the Temple during its consecration (1 Kings 8) and Zechariah's prophecy of a final day when even those who were once enemies of God would celebrate Sukkot—and God's glory would once and for all tabernacle among them (Zechariah 14). When temporal time comes to an end, God will again dwell with humanity the same way he did in Eden.

The prophets spoke of a future day when there would be no more temporary, time-bound sukkot. Ezekiel's vivid vision of a valley of dry bones ends with the promise of God to dwell with his own forever:

> I will make a covenant of peace with them; it will be an
> everlasting covenant. I will establish them and increase
> their numbers, and I will put my sanctuary among them
> forever. My dwelling place will be with them; I will be
> their God, and they will be my people. Then the nations
> will know that I the LORD make Israel holy, when my
> sanctuary is among them forever.   EZEKIEL 37:26-28

According to Scripture, the Feast of Tabernacles is to last seven days (Leviticus 23:34; Numbers 29:12; Deuteronomy 16:15). On the eighth and final day of this festival, the people enjoy a day of rest and rejoicing of the same nature as their weekly Sabbaths. On this final day, known as *Simchat Torah* ("Rejoicing with the Torah"), the cycle of Torah readings for the year begins anew in Genesis 1. We taste the promise of complete restoration and new creation in this final feast day of rest and new beginnings.

GOD WITH US

Followers of Jesus can trace the Feast of Tabernacles through the New Testament. It is not an accident that the Gospel of John uses the language of sukkah, tabernacle, and temple to testify to Jesus: "The Word became flesh and *made his dwelling* [in Greek, *skenoo*, "to tabernacle"] among us. We have seen his glory, the glory of the one and only Son, who came from the Father, full of grace and truth" (John 1:14). Eugene Peterson's paraphrase of this verse in *The Message* offers a contemporary take on the meaning of these words: "The Word became flesh and blood, and moved into the neighborhood." The One who was, is, and always will be moved into the neighborhood with us in order to establish his Kingdom. Sukkot points to the first coming of Jesus, born in a temporary dwelling in Bethlehem. And it promises that he will return to reign over the "neighborhood" he created and came to redeem and restore.

The deeply embedded Sukkot hope for a Messiah to move into the neighborhood informed Peter's blurted response at the Transfiguraton (Luke 9:28-36; Mark 9:2-13). This eternal moment in temporal time gave the three disciples a glimpse of the glory of Jesus, joined by Moses and Elijah, as representatives of the Torah and the Prophets. Was this the end of days? Had heaven come to earth? What was the proper way to welcome these guests? Peter suggested he and James and John build some sukkot: "Master, it is good for us to be here. Let us put up three shelters—one for you, one for Moses and one for Elijah" (Luke 9:33). The word for *shelters* used in this verse is a cousin to *skenoo*. Peter's nervous words reflect his deep longing for God to move into the neighborhood once and for all.

Perhaps just when they thought they could bear no more of this wonder, the glory of God enveloped the group. Instead of responding to Peter's suggestion, the Father affirmed his relationship to Jesus and gave Peter, James, and John their marching orders. It was not time to build a tabernacle and stay on the mountain. "This is my Son, whom I love. Listen to him!" (Mark 9:7). Sukkot's ultimate meaning is yet to be fulfilled.

The apostle Paul uses similar imagery to describe the way in which God was at work in the church, building individuals together to become "a dwelling in which God lives by his Spirit" (Ephesians 2:22). For years I pictured a giant, brick-and-mortar church building when I read these words. My modern sensibilities obscured Paul's context. But each gathering of Jesus' followers in first-century towns and cities functioned as a human tabernacle. Together as a community, they were on mission to proclaim God's presence to those around them. This dwelling of which Paul spoke was not a sanctuary *from* the world but a tabernacle *for* the world.

HOSPITALITY

Sukkot has a powerful present-tense message of hospitality, as well as a future-focused message of hope fulfilled. Sukkot invites us to respond to God's presence in our lives by welcoming others into ours. Deuteronomy 16:13-14 emphasizes this:

> Celebrate the Festival of Tabernacles for seven days after you have gathered the produce of your threshing floor and your winepress. Be joyful at your festival—you, your sons and daughters, your male and female servants, and the Levites, the foreigners, the fatherless and the widows who live in your towns.

Jewish literature traces the theme of hospitality at Sukkot to a time hundreds of years before Moses, when Abraham welcomed three strangers into his tent (Genesis 18:1-15). Those strangers turned out to be supernatural visitors who promised him he would at last become a father. Medieval Jewish philosopher Maimonides describes the abundant delight that characterizes this holiday:

> *When one eats and drinks, one must also feed the stranger,*
> *the orphan, the widow and other unfortunate paupers. But*
> *one who locks the doors of his courtyard, and eat* [sic] *and*
> *drinks with his children and wife but does not feed the poor*
> *and the embittered soul—this is not the joy of a mitzvah* [a
> good deed done out of religious duty], *but the joy of his*
> *belly.*[3]

Jesus told a pair of parables about what true hospitality looks like. Luke 14:1-24 includes the story of guests who flexed their social and religious privilege by hogging the best seats at a banquet and the story of an important man who received excuses instead of presence from the people he'd invited to his party. The outcasts and forgotten people living at the margins of "proper" religious society become the honored guests in both of these stories. Certainly, the application of these stories extends beyond party giving to help Jesus' hearers understand the Kingdom of which he spoke, which has an entirely different economy and social order than the one of the world. But he also demonstrated that the table is where true Kingdom community begins:

> Jesus said to his host, "When you give a luncheon or
> dinner, do not invite your friends, your brothers or sisters,
> your relatives, or your rich neighbors; if you do, they may
> invite you back and so you will be repaid. But when you

give a banquet, invite the poor, the crippled, the lame, the blind, and you will be blessed. Although they cannot repay you, you will be repaid at the resurrection of the righteous." LUKE 14:12-14

These parables aren't referencing Sukkot, of course. Hospitality is a 365-day-per-year proposition. However, Sukkot's focus on feasting gives us a wonderful opportunity to invite others to our table—and may provide a nudge to those who don't exercise their hospitality muscles very often. Our culture has turned hospitality into performance. We can watch beautiful meals being prepared on one basic cable network and tour picture-perfect homes on another. Food and home magazines and restaurant meals have escalated our notions of entertaining beyond simply adding another place setting or three at our kitchen table. The informality of Sukkot (even dining alfresco under a starry sky is a wonderful place to start!) puts the focus on simply sharing our table with family, friends, strangers, and sojourners. As we do, we share our joy in the Lord.

HOPE

The observant Jewish community believes Sukkot is a holiday promising a final, future Messianic fulfillment. While they don't believe that Jesus' first advent launched "the beginning of the end," there are many in the Jewish community who are longing for the final day of ingathering, when people from all nations of God's world will join them to come live in God's presence.

When we as Christ's followers pray, "Your kingdom come, your will be done, on earth as it is in heaven" (Matthew 6:10), we are expressing our hope in Jesus our Pioneer, who told his disciples he'd come to lead us somewhere far more permanent than a sukkah:

Do not let your hearts be troubled. You believe in God; believe also in me. My Father's house has many rooms; if that were not so, would I have told you that I am going there to prepare a place for you? And if I go and prepare a place for you, I will come back and take you to be with me that you also may be where I am. You know the way to the place where I am going. JOHN 14:1-4

They knew the way because they knew Jesus. If he is our hope, he will be our home for eternity.

Hope is our compass while we journey with Jesus as pilgrims through time to his story's conclusion. In the final movement of the book of Revelation, John uses language to describe the end of finite time in a way that echoes Ezekiel's "dry bones" promise. Like Ezekiel, John sees the fulfillment of Sukkot at the end of time, when in Revelation he quotes a voice from the throne declaring that God will forevermore "be with them and be their God" (Revelation 21:3).

In his classic *The Return of the King*, author J. R. R. Tolkien notes that in the end, everything sad will come untrue. No more impermanent dwellings. No more uprooting. No more desert wandering. No more temporary shelters. We will, at last, be home.

EVERYDAY ETERNITY: SUKKOT

One name for Sukkot is the "Feast of Ingathering." While the name certainly stirs images of agricultural harvest time, it actually points forward toward the time when God's people from every tongue, tribe, and nation will be gathered to him (Revelation 5:9). Sukkot invites us to savor each year the sweet promise of ingathering as our penultimate family reunion.

If your family or small group is interested in a Sukkot experience, planning a casual harvest-themed potluck is a simple way to begin. Make sure your feast includes reciting some or all of Psalms 113–118 together. And invite a few people from outside your usual circle to join you around your table.

If you live in a town with a synagogue in it, why not see if you can make arrangements to visit their congregational sukkah? The experience of standing inside of one will give you a far better picture of the holiday's central image than words can.

Your family, small group, or children's Sunday school class may want to try building a sukkah. You can search online for some simple building and decorating instructions.

And rejoice! Our King is coming to dwell with us forever!

9

STONES OF REMEMBRANCE

Jewish History's Holy Days

GOD'S WORK among the Jewish people has continued throughout history. During the last two thousand years, the Jewish people have experienced anew the story of God's redemption as they've walked through the yearly feast cycle. Rabbis and sages marked miraculous accounts of his faithfulness on the calendar in much the same way that Joshua and the children of Israel set up stones of remembrance as they crossed into the Promised Land (Joshua 4). That stacked boulder memorial served as a way for fathers to tell their children the story of God parting the waters of the Jordan River, allowing the people to pass through to the other side—and for their children to pass on the story to future generations.

"Stones of remembrance" have been placed in the Jewish calendar to mark other major historical events that happened in the life of the Jewish people. These include the destruction of the first and second Temples in Jerusalem, the Babylonian captivity, the stunning defeat of a pagan king who'd desecrated the Temple, and the founding of the modern state of Israel.

The feasts described in Leviticus 23 are tied to the Exodus. These other red-letter days on the Jewish calendar mark later events in the story of the Hebrew people. Some, like Chanukah, are fairly well known in Gentile culture. Others have been minor celebrations rooted primarily within religious Jewish culture. Still others have become opportunities for education among both Jews and Gentiles about contemporary Jewish issues. Here's a brief look at some of the other rabbinic and modern holidays on the Jewish calendar.

CHANUKAH

The story of Chanukah, found in the apocryphal books of 1–2 Maccabees, is not included in either Jewish or Protestant Bibles. Catholic and Orthodox Christian Bibles include these books, which detail the heroism of a Jewish priest named Matthias. He took refuge in the Judean hills west of Jerusalem after a wave of persecution by the Seleucid (Greek) king Antiochus IV Epiphanes. In 175 BC, Matthias gathered a band of holy warriors around him to reclaim and cleanse the Temple from Seleucid control. These warriors came to be known as the Maccabees, a name likely derived from the Hebrew nickname given to Matthias's ferocious son Judah, "the Hammer."

In 164 BC, the Maccabees regained control of the Temple in Jerusalem. The priests who entered the defiled space immediately set to work reconsecrating it for worship to God. They were glad to find enough pure oil to relight the Temple's lampstand (described in detail in Exodus 25:31-40; also called the menorah). However, oral history from the period recounts that though there was only enough fuel for one day, the lamp's flame burned for eight miraculous days, which gave the Maccabees enough time to prepare a fresh supply. Seeing the light burn once again in the holy place after years of darkness and idol worship must have been pure joy for Judah and company. The celebration of this victory became Chanukah, also known as the "Festival of Lights."

The Temple remained in worshipping Jewish hands for the next two centuries. Because of this, when Jesus was born, Joseph and Mary were able to consecrate their newly circumcised infant son in the Temple (see Exodus 13:2, 12). The miracle of Chanukah made this possible.

At the time of Christ, the festival was a minor Jewish holiday during the first century. It's mentioned in John 10:22. The holiday teaches about the nature of courage in the acts of the priests-turned-warriors. Judah and the Maccabees were driven by their desire to worship God as he'd called them to do, free from oppression by pagan rulers.

Chanukah in modern culture has been elevated to kind of a "Jewish Christmas." The holiday is celebrated by lighting a special nine-branched lampstand (commonly referred to as a menorah, though its official name is *chanukiah*). On each of the eight nights of the festival, families light one candle and add it to the chanukiah. The ninth branch on the chanukiah is for the candle used to kindle the rest.

Many kids receive gifts each night of the holiday. When I was growing up, the really cool toys were given as gifts on the first, second, and (sometimes) last night. The other days featured less inspiring gifts, such as pajamas or underwear. The Chanukah menu includes fried foods such as potato pancakes and jelly donuts, a tasty nod to the miracle of the oil lasting in the Temple's menorah.

TU B'SHVAT

Tu B'Shvat ("TOO bi-sheh-VAHT") is a midwinter holiday known as the new year for trees. Named after the date and month of the celebration, it is the time of year in Israel when the trees start budding. Leviticus 19:23-25 prohibited the people from eating of a tree's fruit for the first three years of its existence. In the fourth year, that tree's produce would be an offering to the Lord. The people were free to use its fruit for themselves from the fifth year forward. Tu B'Shvat thus became a way to mark the beginning of a new year in order to calculate Temple offerings for the trees of the land.[1]

Christians can see the imprint of this commandment in the parable Jesus told about the barren fig tree in Luke 13:6-9. The tree's owner wanted to cut down his fig tree after it hadn't produced any fruit for three years. He was stopped by the intercession of the vineyard's caretaker. In light of the commandment in Leviticus, the desire by the tree's owner to cut it down demonstrates impatience and his desire to circumvent God's timing and provision.

In the Jewish community today, Tu B'Shvat is known as a sort of "Jewish Arbor Day." When I was a child, we collected money to be used by the Jewish National Fund for the planting of trees in Israel to commemorate this holiday.[2] The first time I visited Israel I was forty-seven years old. I saw the forests of beautiful mature trees in the country and thought of the little seedlings my quarters had helped to purchase decades earlier. The trees blooming in the desert landscape reminded me of the prophetic promise from Isaiah 35:1-2:

> The desert and the parched land will be glad;
> the wilderness will rejoice and blossom.

Like the crocus, it will burst into bloom;
　　it will rejoice greatly and shout for joy.
The glory of Lebanon will be given to it,
　　the splendor of Carmel and Sharon;
they will see the glory of the LORD,
　　the splendor of our God.

PURIM

Purim ("puh-RIM") retells the story of how brave, beautiful Esther and her wise cousin Mordecai saved the Jewish people from an ancient holocaust during the time of the Exile, five centuries before the birth of Christ. Costumes and parties allow the Jewish community an opportunity to honor the God whose fingerprints are all over this story of salvation.

This late-winter feast is focused around the reading of the book of Esther. This is not a time for solemnity, however. The reading takes on the air of a melodrama: Villain Haman's name is booed every time it's read. This is the most unbuttoned and zany day of the Jewish calendar—a day for costumes, parties, games, and (for adults) drinking. The revelry is reminiscent of the way in which Halloween or Mardi Gras is celebrated in modern American culture.

Beyond the partying, however, Purim has a very serious message: What could have been a genocide of the Jewish people during their captivity in Persia was short-circuited by the courage of Esther and Mordecai.

HOLOCAUST REMEMBRANCE DAY

In 2005 the United Nations declared January 27 International Holocaust Remembrance Day. The commemoration serves as one part memorial and one part opportunity for education about the World War II genocide that killed nearly two-thirds of Europe's Jews, as well as an additional five to six million other people, including the disabled, homosexuals, and the Romani (gypsy) people, who were deemed unfit to live in Adolf Hitler's "racially pure" vision of a new Europe.

The Jewish community set aside a different day for remembering the Jewish victims of the Holocaust. Established in 1953, this springtime holiday is part of a civil cycle of observance that marks the birth of the modern state of Israel. Yom HaShoah (literally, Day of Catastrophe) is the first of these civil observances and takes place each year two weeks after Passover.

There have been other genocides in the twentieth century, each horrifying in its own right. Yet the scope and focus of the Holocaust remains a unique event in history. Nobel Peace Prize winner and author Elie Wiesel, himself a survivor of the Nazi death camps, once said, "To forget the dead would be akin to killing them a second time."[3] Yom HaShoah gives us an opportunity to remember. It also offers Christians an important opportunity to listen to, learn from, and mourn with the Jewish community.

Out of the ashes of the Holocaust, the modern state of Israel was born, and several Israeli civil holidays are associated with it. Yom HaShoah is followed by Yom HaZikaron, enacted into law in 1963. Each spring Israel's Memorial Day commemorates the country's fallen military heroes. The following day is Israel Independence Day (Yom HaAtzma'ut), a day marked in Israel much like July 4 is in the United States, with many Israelis gathering with friends and family for picnics and trips to the beach.

The final springtime civil holiday is Yom Yerushalayim

(Jerusalem Day), which marks the reunification of the city of Jerusalem at the conclusion of the Six Day War in 1967.

TISHA B'AV

Tisha B'Av is the saddest day of the entire Jewish year. The religiously observant community participates in this midsummer day of mourning and fasting, which marks the destruction of both the first and second Temples in ancient Jerusalem in 586 BC and AD 70, respectively. The date has been the eerie anniversary of a number of other tragedies throughout history that have befallen the Jewish people since that time, including the crushing of the Bar Kochba revolt (AD 132), the launching of the devastating First Crusade (1095), the expulsion of the Jews from England (1290) and later Spain (1492), and the beginning of mass deportations from the Warsaw Ghetto in Poland to the Nazi concentration camps (1942).[4]

ETERNAL MOMENTS WORTH MARKING

The Jewish historical holidays honor the way in which God has continued to work among his people through and beyond the events canonized in Scripture. The stones of remembrance that mark the Jewish calendar allow us to engage with the experiences of those who have come before us and to celebrate God's continuing faithfulness:

> I will remember the deeds of the LORD;
> yes, I will remember your miracles of long ago.
> I will consider all your works
> and meditate on all your mighty deeds.

PSALM 77:11-12

These holidays remind all of us, Jew and Gentile alike, that pilgrimage through time is not limited to the length of our own life spans. The trail blazed by those who have come before us includes eternal moments worth marking for reasons both negative and positive. Their suffering is hallowed in our lives as we determine to "never forget." The act of remembering God's "mighty deeds" connects the past with our present. By allowing the calendar's stones of remembrance to do their work in our lives, we are numbering our days in ways that will teach us to walk in perseverance, worship, and yes, wisdom.

Throughout the Scriptures, God called on the Jewish people to remember who they were—beloved pilgrim people, called to reflect his light to the world—and whose they were: his. And it was in the fullness of time, at just the right moment in history, that the eternal God sent his beloved Son to do for fallen humanity— both Jew and Gentile—what we could never, ever do for ourselves:

> When the set time had fully come, God sent his Son,
> born of a woman, born under the law, to redeem those
> under the law, that we might receive adoption to sonship.
> . . . So you are no longer a slave, but God's child; and
> since you are his child, God has made you also an heir.
>
> GALATIANS 4:4-7

In other words, God remembered us. Jesus fulfilled the Law with his life, death, and resurrection. In doing so, he filled full the salvation story of the feasts, deleting nothing while changing everything. For the lion's share of his followers over the last two millennia, that included the calendar.

PART TWO

The Christian Calendar

10

FROM HERE TO THERE

Introduction to the Christian Calendar

THE WOMEN MADE THEIR WAY out of the city just as the rim of the sun edged over the jagged horizon. Burial spice-scent rose from bundles in their arms like incensed prayer. They made their way to the temporary tomb where their beloved Master's bloodied, dead body had been laid two days earlier.

Pilate had posted guards outside the tomb to ensure no one tampered with the body (Matthew 27:62-65). After all, there'd been all sorts of troubling talk from Jesus and his followers about resurrection. Having heard that Jesus brought Lazarus back to life after four days in the grave (John 11), Pilate was taking no chances.

The women would need help to move the impossibly heavy stone covering the cave, a temporary grave provided by Joseph of Arimathea, so they could prepare Jesus' body for permanent burial. They found the guards unharmed but unconscious, flat on the cold ground. Two lightning-bright beings met the women with words that split human history in two:

Why do you look for the living among the dead? He is
not here; he has risen! Remember how he told you, while
he was still with you in Galilee: "The Son of Man must be
delivered over to the hands of sinners, be crucified and on
the third day be raised again." LUKE 24:5-7

Civilizations touched by the Good News would come to mark
this event by dividing time in relation to Jesus Christ: BC (before
Christ's birth) and AD (*anno Domini*, Latin for "in the year of the
Lord"). Modern academic, scientific, secular, and Jewish publications prefer the alternative abbreviations BCE (before the Common
or Christian Era) and CE (Common or Christian Era). But even
these abbreviations still count time from the advent of Christ:
AD 1959 and 1959 CE both refer to 1,959 years after Jesus' birth.

But before anyone began to consider how to mark time, the
believing community first had to learn to live an AD reality. Less
than two months after the Resurrection, between Passover and
Shavuot, the community of disciples had swelled from a few hand-
fuls of wonderstruck friends of Jesus to a Holy Spirit–empowered
community of more than three thousand (Acts 2). This new community was marked by signs, wonders, deep generosity, social
boundary–shattering hospitality, and rapid numerical growth.

While the predominately Jewish early church continued to
gather at the Temple and observe the weekly Sabbath and yearly festal cycle, their everyday gatherings with other followers of Jesus took
place primarily in homes and gradually fell into a rhythm centered
on the first day of the week. Sunday, the day of the Resurrection,
defined them as Jesus people (Acts 20:7).

Sunday had long served Jews as both a marker of the first day
of creation and the promise of the new creation that would be

ushered in by the Messiah. An "eighth day" of new beginnings had been embedded into the Jewish pilgrim feasts from the start. Functionally, one night of Passover followed immediately by the seven nights of the Feast of Unleavened Bread was a single eight-day holiday. The holiday of Shavuot/Pentecost came on the fiftieth day after Passover, at the beginning of the eighth week. The fall Feast of Tabernacles was eight days long. The number eight, then, was a reminder that Messiah would come one day to make right everything in this fallen world.

This Messianic hope had been with the Jewish community from the beginning. Some expected that a renewed Israel would become a national fulfillment of that hope. Many others were looking for a political leader. Instead, God sent his Son.

FIRST DAY, EIGHTH DAY

The significance of the Resurrection occurring on the first day of the week was not lost on believers during the early decades of the church. It was the beginning of the new beginning. Sundays became for the early church a way to both remember and to proclaim to the world around them that they were eighth-day people. One of the Gentile leaders of the era, Ignatius of Antioch, described the eighth-day worship customs of the church in his city: "They . . . order their lives by the Lord's Day . . . the Day when life first dawned for us, thanks to Him and His death."[1] The *Didache* ("di-DAH-kee"), a document likely written between AD 50 and 120 outlines doctrine and practice among the early church and makes note of the growing importance of Sunday as a day of worship: "On the Lord's own day gather yourselves together and break bread and give thanks, first confessing your transgressions, that your sacrifice may be pure."[2]

Eighth-day living came with its challenges. Leaders of the first-century church had wrestled through what it would look like for Gentiles to join what had been a mostly Jewish movement.

While Jesus aimed his ministry at seeking the lost sheep of Israel (Matthew 15:21-28), he did so with the expectation that his found sheep would carry his message of salvation to all the nations (Matthew 5:14-16; 28:16-20). Eventually, in response to increasing numbers of Gentiles coming into their congregations, the early followers of Jesus settled on a very brief list of behavioral prohibitions: "You are to abstain from food sacrificed to idols, from blood, from the meat of strangled animals and from sexual immorality." This limited "burden" on the Gentiles "seemed good to the Holy Spirit and to us" (Acts 15:28-29).

For most of the first century AD, mainstream Jews tolerated the Jesus-following Jews among them as a sect. In the chaos and dispersion that followed the destruction of the Temple in AD 70, however, a chasm began to form between the two groups. As the dispersed Jewish community tried to figure out how to survive without a land, king, or Temple, religious leaders clamped down on those sects that didn't fit their increasingly rigid definitions of orthodoxy. Jews began to distance themselves from their Jewish brothers and sisters who proclaimed that Jesus was the Messiah.

The young church did plenty of distancing of its own from the Jewish community as well. By the beginning of the second century, the church had taken root among the pagan peoples ringing the Mediterranean and in Europe, northern Africa, and western Asia. The numbers and proportion of Gentiles grew exponentially in these young congregations, and the church began to disconnect from its Jewish foundations.

One of the first major breaks the young church had with the Jews happened as believers began to wrestle with how to celebrate the resurrection of Jesus. The yearly feast of Passover became, for the early Christian community, a way to commemorate the ultimate act of Jesus' life on earth. Greek-speaking believers called the feast *Pasch*, a translation of the Hebrew *Pesach* (Passover). Christians clashed over which date each year they'd celebrate in order to distinguish their celebration from the Passover of the Jews.

There were two camps: those who believed the Christian Pasch should stay on the fourteenth day of Nisan (the start of Passover) and those who believed the Pasch needed to be separated from the Jewish feast day. Both sides wanted to communicate a distinctly Christian message: For the former, Jesus was the true Paschal Lamb, and thus his followers were the true Chosen People; for the latter, Jesus' resurrection was a triumph not only over the grave but also over all religious customs and rules.[3]

To modern ears, haggling over a calendar date may sound like a petty thing, but it flowed out of a fierce debate that did not end with the resolution in Acts 15. Galatians 2 details Paul's dispute with those who insisted that believing Gentiles needed to follow Jewish Law. You can hear Paul's frustration in verse 14:

When I saw that they were not acting in line with the truth of the gospel, I said to Cephas [Peter] in front of them all, "You are a Jew, yet you live like a Gentile and not like a Jew. How is it, then, that you force Gentiles to follow Jewish customs?"

Ultimately, the only two major Jewish feasts that "crossed over" to the Gentile Christian community were Passover and Shavuot/

Pentecost. No other feast days were adapted from the Jewish calendar to correlate to any of the other key events in the life of Jesus.

FROM OUTLAWED FAITH TO THE LAW OF THE EMPIRE

Neither did early church leaders seem to feel a need to create new dates or seasons at this point. Three centuries of persecution kept the church looking to the future, watching and waiting for the return of Jesus, when all injustice would come to an end. The simplicity of the church's worship was forged out of its outlaw status: Christianity was a rebel sect, increasingly removed from Judaism and yet rejected by the Roman Empire—until AD 313, when Emperor Constantine decreed it to be Rome's official religion.

Historians continue to debate whether Constantine experienced a true personal conversion to Christ or whether he embraced Christianity to further his own political ends. In any case, with the stroke of his pen (or quill, as the case may be), Constantine's decree radically changed the way in which the church saw itself.

Constantine discovered that the church was divided over matters of doctrine and practice. Threats and counterthreats of excommunication continued until Emperor Constantine convened a council of church leaders at Nicaea (located in modern Turkey) in AD 325 to hack through issues of doctrine and practice.[4] The Nicene council determined that Pasch would never be celebrated on the fourteenth of Nisan, even if it fell on a Sunday. Instead, it would be held on the first Sunday after the first full moon occurring on or after the vernal equinox.[5]

One thing was certain: Whether advocating for celebrating the Resurrection alongside the Passover or lobbying against it, the early Christians were increasingly anxious to differentiate themselves from the Jews. With its formal adoption by the Roman Empire,

Christianity was quickly empowered to finally sever its relationship to Judaism—an act not unlike a branch cutting itself off of a tree. Church historian Oskar Skarsaune noted another effect of Constantine's actions:

> *Instead of looking forward to being released from the world, Christians began to think that they were to stay in the world and Christianize it, conquer it. Worship developed a different orientation; instead of being mainly future-oriented, it began looking back to the decisive events of salvation history, it became "historicized." In the weekly services of Sunday morning the whole of biblical history was retold and liturgically reenacted, especially the story of Christ, but gradually also the entire biblical history from creation to new Jerusalem.*[6]

By the fourth century, the church had ritualized preparation for Pasch with formal fasting and prayer. This special Sunday became a day for baptism, a beautiful reenactment of resurrection life. The week after, Pasch was given over to additional instruction for those who had been newly baptized. Within a couple more generations, the events of Jesus' final week were given specific days of commemoration in the week leading up to Pasch. The fifty days following the Resurrection Day observance were their own cycle of anticipation and observance leading up to Pentecost, including a worship service and readings in remembrance of Jesus' ascension on day forty.

And a new Christian holiday was added to the year. In the fourth century, Christ's birth found its way onto the official church calendar, commemorated each year on December 25. Where the spring cycles of Pasch-Pentecost were still tied to the lunar calendar used by the Jews, Christmas was tied to the solar (Julian) calendar of the Roman Empire. The Christian holy days thus took on the shape of the Nicene Creed, moving directly from the birth of Christ to his death, resurrection, and ascension (and the outpouring of the Holy Spirit on Pentecost). While other holy days and seasons were added over time, this basic structure formed the foundation of the Christian year still in use by the church today.

LIGHTS AND CRUMBS

I may not have known the exact date of Christmas when I was a child, but after I came to faith in Jesus as Messiah during my teens, I couldn't wait to see what the Christian hubbub was about. My parents forbade me from attending church as long as I lived under their roof, so my first three Christmases as a believer were spent alone in my room, reading my Bible and listening to Christmas carols on the radio. I figured that the tree, lights, presents, carols, and maybe even Santa had something to do with the birth of Jesus. I couldn't wait to try out this Christian holiday for myself.

The first year my husband and I were married, I decided to surprise him by setting up my first-ever Christmas tree. While he was at work, I headed to a local tree lot and purchased a half-barren, lopsided ball of a spruce tree, a tree stand, and a couple of strings of lights on white cords. (I had no idea that white cords were for houses and green cords were for Christmas trees. Yes, our tree looked as pathetic as you're imagining it did.)

The holiday decorating, baking, parties, and special services at church were pleasant enough, but they didn't lead me to the manger to worship the baby King like I thought they would. It didn't take me long to recognize that my lonely first Christmases, without all the cultural trappings, had been far more worshipful than these busywork-packed ones.

This led to an aha! moment for me. The Jewish calendar was countercultural, a way for the Chosen People to live a different story than their pagan neighbors were living. It was one obvious way in which they reflected and magnified God's light to the nations. The building blocks of the Christian calendar came from the same place, but as Christianity had become mainstream across Europe, the Middle East, western Asia, and parts of northern Africa, its calendar became less countercultural, more a mere timekeeper for the culture. Its prophetic purpose was diluted by its popularity.

The Christian calendar's adoption by the majority culture has had some funny effects on the worship patterns of many modern churches. For years, my husband and I attended nondenominational churches that treated Christmas and Easter as evangelism events. Few considered that by approaching Christianity's holy days in such a similar way as their commemorations of civil or cultural holidays—Mother's Day, Father's Day, Thanksgiving, Memorial Day—they might be allowing culture to shape our worship rather than the other way around. It's ironic that while we have debated for a generation about worship music styles and preferences, I can't remember anyone ever questioning how our calendar affects our worship, forms our identity as followers of Christ, or calls us to live on mission in any way counter to popular culture. Few in the evangelical world have asked how we in the church might learn to number our days so we'd cultivate a heart of wisdom.

Eventually, I became involved in planning worship services for one such congregation. As I researched resources and sought counsel from worship planners and leaders in other churches, I discovered a vast storehouse of riches in the historical liturgies, prayers, and rituals of the church. And some of those rituals bore the imprints of the Jewish holy days I'd known as child.

Much of contemporary evangelicalism has been quick to "put the cookies on the bottom shelf," eschewing the church's history and traditions so that spiritual seekers would feel welcome in our midst. In the process, I wonder if we have gotten used to dining on crumbs. Crumbs may fill us for a moment, but we have been made for eternity; our calendar tells us so.

On the other hand, churches that closely follow the historic Christian calendar can sometimes settle for crumbs of a different flavor. The yearly cycle of practice can become rote and lifeless, and the scripted nature of formal church liturgy can become a monotone religious activity for participants—and a befuddling challenge for visitors.

At its best, the church year can help followers of Jesus know and live his story. It can be used to cultivate discipleship and shape worship. It invites us to the intersection of history and eternity.

THE CHRISTIAN YEAR

Each day and season in the Christian year moves us through the main events in Jesus' life and ministry. But the Christian year is not merely an annual memorial tour. It is meant to be a way to help us remember we are living eternity every day. There are eight main seasons in the Christian calendar.

Advent is a time of preparation during the four weeks leading up to Christmas. Advent typically has a dual focus: readying hearts to welcome the incarnate Son of Man into our midst and prompting Jesus' followers to look forward with anticipation to the day of his return to earth as the reigning Son of God.

Christmas begins on December 25.[7] This twelve-day season is focused on the mystery and miracle of the birth of Jesus.

Epiphany is a season focused on revelation: Christ to the Gentiles (represented by the magi's visit) and the relationship of Christ to the Father and Spirit at his baptism.

Lent is a forty-day season of repentance beginning on Ash Wednesday and continuing through Holy Week.

While *Holy Week* is counted as part of Lent, it is a central focus of the Christian year. Each day of this week commemorates a different aspect of Jesus' final week.

Easter is a season celebrating the resurrection of Jesus, beginning on Resurrection Sunday (Easter) and continuing through Pentecost.

Pentecost rejoices in the giving of the Holy Spirit in Acts 2. It marks a turning point in the church year, as the Spirit-empowered church symbolically moves out into the world.

Ordinary Time doesn't signify "average" or "mundane" time. Instead, it is a reference to the ordinal numbers (first, second, third, and so on) used to count the weeks given to the church's Spirit-empowered work in the world. This long season stretches from early summer through the end of November. Christ the King Sunday, which celebrates his victorious reign and is the final Sunday of Ordinary Time, brings the Christian year to its conclusion.

Author Lawrence Hull Stookey offers a vivid picture of how living at the intersection of history and eternity can shape our lives:

The Christian story reaches back to the Exodus of ancient Israel and before and stretches forward to the descent of a new heaven and a new earth and beyond. Indeed, it can be said that Christians are called to assume a cruciform posture: Standing upright with feet firmly planted in the present, we stretch out one arm to grasp our heritage and the other arm to lay hold of our hope; standing thus, we assume the shape of our central symbol of faith: the cross. If either hand releases its grip, spiritual disaster threatens as the sign of the cross becomes misformed.[8]

When we reach out through the rhythms of the Christian year to hold on to our heritage and our hope, we may find that he who is our heritage and our hope is the One holding us.

11

LONGING FOR HOME

Advent

THE EMOTIONAL AND SPIRITUAL TONE of Advent, the first season of the Christian year, can be found in words written more than five centuries before the birth of Jesus.

In 586 BC, Jerusalem and the surrounding territory of Judah fell to the Babylonians. Most of the able-bodied people of Judah were marched hundreds of miles across the Fertile Crescent and forcibly resettled in Babylon.

The Jews were a spiritually, morally, and militarily compromised people by the time they were conquered by the Babylonians. Through both the Torah God had given them at Sinai and the warnings of the prophets he'd sent over the years, God had alerted them to the consequences of compromise. Scripture passages like Deuteronomy 13:5, 1 Samuel 12:14-15, Psalm 2:10-12, and Isaiah 1:1-25 are just a few examples of the consistent, firm warnings God gave his Chosen People about indulging and accommodating sin. The Babylonian captivity, however, was the ultimate consequence: the first time Judah had been displaced from the land since Joshua had led them there many generations earlier.

Far from home, an unnamed scribe wrote these words of lament:

By the rivers of Babylon we sat and wept
   when we remembered Zion.
There on the poplars
   we hung our harps,
for there our captors asked us for songs,
   our tormentors demanded songs of joy;
   they said, "Sing us one of the songs of Zion!"

How can we sing the songs of the LORD
   while in a foreign land?
If I forget you, Jerusalem,
   may my right hand forget its skill.
May my tongue cling to the roof of my mouth
   if I do not remember you,
if I do not consider Jerusalem
   my highest joy.

PSALM 137:1-6

The Babylonians expected that the disorienting humiliation of being uprooted from Judea and relegated to third-class, noncitizen status would break the spirits of the Jews. Instead, as God intended, it purged the Chosen People of their sin and focused their hopes on the God who'd once delivered them from Egyptian slavery and promised through his prophets to bring them home again to live under his reign. After seventy years in captivity, the Jewish people were allowed to return to their land under the rule of a series of foreign kings. They were still far from the kind of home their forefathers had known; they still waited for their deliverance.

This kind of watching, longing, and waiting is what Advent is meant to be. Advent directs our desires toward God's promise of a Redeemer. The word *advent* means "arrival" or "coming."

THE ADVENT OF ADVENT

When John the Baptist burst onto the scene, he preached repentance, then immersed all those who responded in the Jordan River as a sign of their "all in" commitment. He was living out the prophetic promise that a forerunner would herald the arrival of a saving Ruler (Isaiah 40:3; Luke 3:3). John's message was simple: Get ready. Stay ready. Your King is coming.

The first season of the Christian year prepares us to accept God's gift of his only Son. We do so by humbling ourselves in repentance and confessing our need for his salvation. Connecting with our longing for salvation as spiritual exiles is the "why" of Advent. John's message and ministry focus is the "how."

Advent followed the fourth century AD adoption of Christmas as being celebrated on December 25. Christmas was the first Christian holiday anchored in the solar calendar, used throughout the Roman Empire. The spring feast cycle of Easter–Pentecost remained tied to the lunar calendar and their Jewish holy day equivalents.

Along with Easter and Pentecost, Christmas was one of the times during the year when new believers were baptized. At first, Advent was the period in which these new believers received instruction about the faith. During this time of preparation, some church members also fasted and prayed for these new members.[1] The time of spiritual preparation varied from three to six weeks. Eventually, Western (Roman) church leaders added a four-week Advent season to the calendar, while Eastern (Orthodox) church leaders decreed a forty-day period of fasting (not including

Sundays) that began each year in mid-November. By the beginning of the eighth century, Advent was recognized as the beginning of the church year.[2]

Though the original focus of Advent was on preparing church members to welcome the newborn Jesus on Christmas, the season eventually came to have an equally strong focus on the second coming of Christ. Church leaders recognized that the theme of spiritual readiness applied just as strongly to the birth of the Messiah as to his promised, triumphant return.

PEOPLE, GET READY

One of the oldest prayer traditions of Advent is the recitation of a group of prayers called the O Antiphons. This cycle of ancient prayers is a part of the Western church's liturgy during the final week of Advent leading up to Christmas Eve. They likely date to the seventh or eighth century and are drawn from key prophetic passages found in the book of Isaiah. A sung or chanted verse serving as part of a liturgical response in prayer, each O Antiphon begins with the cry "O!" and ends by asking the Messiah to come.

> › *December 17:* "O Wisdom, you come forth from the mouth of the Most High. You fill the universe and hold all things together in a strong yet gentle manner. O come to teach us the way of truth." (Isaiah 11:2-3; 28:29)
> › *December 18:* "O Adonai and leader of Israel, you appeared to Moses in a burning bush and you gave him the Law on Sinai. O come and save us with your mighty power." (Isaiah 11:4-5; 33:22)
> › *December 19:* "O stock of Jesse, you stand as a signal for the nations; kings fall silent before you whom the peoples

acclaim. O come to deliver us, and do not delay." (Isaiah 11:1, 10)

› *December 20:* "O key of David and scepter of Israel, what you open no one else can close again; what you close no one can open. O come to lead the captive from prison; free those who sit in darkness and in the shadow of death." (Isaiah 9:6; 22:22)

› *December 21:* "O Rising Sun, you are the splendor of eternal light and the sun of justice. O come and enlighten those who sit in darkness and in the shadow of death." (Isaiah 9:1)

› *December 22:* "O King whom all the peoples desire, you are the cornerstone which makes all one. O come and save man whom you made from clay." (Isaiah 2:4; 9:5)

› *December 23:* "O Emmanuel, you are our king and judge, the One whom the peoples await and their Savior. O come and save us, Lord, our God." (Isaiah 7:14)[3]

Many congregations light candles during Advent, adding a candle each Sunday throughout the season. The first week's candle typically represents expectation, or the sure promise of a coming Savior. The themes of the remaining three weeks vary from year to year and differ among various Christian traditions. The candles and the evergreen wreath in which they're placed likely have their origins in pagan Germanic midwinter festivals; they were adapted for worship sometime in the Middle Ages.[4] The third Sunday of the four-week Advent cycle, known as Gaudete (Latin for "rejoice") Sunday, lightens the otherwise somber mood of Advent.

A newer corporate worship tradition that's become a cherished part of Advent is a special service called Lessons and Carols. This service uses a combination of Scripture readings and carefully selected carols to point people toward Jesus. The Lessons and

Carols service was first performed in England at King's College, Cambridge, in 1918. The BBC broadcasts the service annually.[5] Many Anglican churches stage their own version of the service. Other churches stage Christmas pageants and plays during this season as an outreach to the community.

Families and individuals have created all kinds of ways in which they observe the Advent season. Some families have enjoyed decorating a small Jesse Tree. Each day of Advent, a family member adds to the tree an ornament or symbol representing an Old Testament prophecy about the coming Messiah, a portrait or name of an Old Testament ancestor found in Jesus' "family tree" (Matthew 1:1-16; Luke 3:23-38), or simply a symbol depicting the Christian faith. Other families incorporate Advent calendars, read special devotionals, or focus on doing acts of generosity and service.

The same commercial creep that brings Christmas decorations into stores as soon as school starts has moved into Advent. Now we can "celebrate" Advent with

> Advent vodka calendars—a different little bottle of vodka (or whiskey, or gin, or cognac) for each day of December leading up to Christmas;
> Advent nail polish calendars—one new fashion color for each day of the last month of the year; and
> LEGO Advent calendars—a toy a day leading up to, presumably, even more LEGO gifts under the tree.[6]

While such lighthearted countdown calendars are meant to be fun, I can imagine that our fathers and mothers in the faith would be pretty surprised to discover we're observing Advent with gifts of daily nail polish.

When my three kids were young, we purchased a children's Advent calendar with Bible verses hiding behind little paper doors. Each child took a turn opening the little doors each evening as a simple way to count through the season. We also got involved in various ministries that provided clothing and gifts for families in need, both locally and overseas. I discovered, however, that it wasn't the practices we added to our family's life that most formed our experience of Advent but what we attempted to subtract or minimize. Choosing to do less created space in our family to learn what it meant to connect with our longing for what—or rather, for *Who*—matters most.

The weeks leading up to Christmas Day in our culture are a frenzied pile-on of frantic activity and consumer spending. There will always be December holiday parties and Christmas programs to fill our schedules. But as often as possible, when a new event or obligation pops up and tries to muscle its way into my date book, I ask myself if there's any way I can postpone it until after December 25. I've penciled in days to take retreat time during this season as well. Advent may be the most countercultural thing we can do during December.

EVERYDAY ETERNITY: ADVENT

There are numerous Advent resources for individuals, families, and congregations, but perhaps the best place to begin is by contemplating what matters most in life. Robert Webber asks a series of questions that we can use throughout Advent to clarify our longings and recalibrate us toward repentance:

> *Do I really believe in Christ? Have I put my hope and trust in him? Do I see the future through the eyes of the one who came*

to redeem the world from the power of evil? Is there a longing within me for him to be formed within, to take up residence in my personal life, in my home, and in my vocation?[7]

One of the best-known carols sung alongside the O Antiphons captures the longing of Advent. The words to "O Come, O Come, Emmanuel" capture the longing of a people living far from home who understood their desires and recognized their need before God:

> O come, O come, Emmanuel,
> And ransom captive Israel
> That mourns in lonely exile here
> Until the Son of God appear.
>
> O come, thou Rod of Jesse, free
> Thine own from Satan's tyranny;
> From depths of hell thy people save,
> And give them victory o'er the grave.
>
> O come, thou Day-spring, come and cheer
> Our spirits by thine advent here;
> Disperse the gloomy clouds of night,
> And death's dark shadows put to flight.
>
> O come, thou key of David, come,
> And open wide our heavenly home;
> Make safe the way that leads on high,
> And close the path to misery.
>
> O come, O come, thou Lord of might,
> Who to thy tribes, on Sinai's height,

In ancient times did'st give the Law,
In cloud, and majesty and awe.

Rejoice! Rejoice! Emmanuel
Shall come to thee, O Israel.

12

WELCOMING THE WORD
MADE FLESH

Christmas

OUR CULTURE'S ANNUAL CHRISTMAS FRENZY begins in mid-October and builds to a peak by the final few days before the holiday at the end of December. After the slate of parties, concerts, present buying, cookie baking, seasonal movie viewing, and holiday-themed events wraps up, the lion's share of the country shuts down. By late afternoon on December 24, we all stagger across the finish line into Christmas.

An eerie hush falls across our culture for about a day and a half as many businesses and restaurants close for the holiday. It's as close to a Jerusalem Sabbath as we'll encounter here. The once-a-year pause in our schedules carries the weight of nostalgia, expectation of perfect gifts, and the hope of happy family gatherings. Mix in the challenge for followers of Jesus to remember "the reason for the season," and Christmas becomes even more complicated. How can you justify "Rockin' around the Christmas Tree" when it's supposed to be a "Silent Night"? How can we balance modern Christmas expectations and demands while worshipping alongside a handful of nameless shepherds at the manger in Bethlehem?

Maybe a single day isn't the answer.

The Christian calendar follows Advent with a Christmas *season*. It stretches beyond the one-day overload of food, family, and presents for twelve days—from December 25 through January 6—to allow us the space to contemplate the mystery and miracle of the One who came to dwell with us. For the Christian calendar, Christmas doesn't end on Christmas Day. It begins there.

ORIGINS

The Gospel of John introduces Jesus to its readers by anchoring him in the story of creation. Jesus was the uncreated One, at once fully human and fully divine. John uses a familiar Jewish metaphor to describe Jesus: "The Word became flesh and made his dwelling among us. We have seen his glory, the glory of the one and only Son, who came from the Father, full of grace and truth" (John 1:14). The words "made his dwelling among us" suggest the Feast of Tabernacles language of *sukkot* (booths), *mishkan* (tabernacle), and the holy Temple. God coming to dwell with his created ones was the heartbeat of the fall holiday of Sukkot.

When the angel told Joseph that his betrothed, Mary, was carrying a child conceived by the Holy Spirit, the angel referenced a prophecy first given to Isaiah hundreds of years earlier that this Son should be named Jesus and would be described as "Immanuel," which meant "God with us" (Isaiah 7:14; Matthew 1:21-23). God himself had indeed tabernacled among them, and he continues to dwell with his community of followers to this day.

Though Scripture situates many events of Jesus' ministry in the Jewish calendar, it does not explicitly tell us when Jesus was born. The early church didn't focus on marking a birth date, and the first few generations of believers focused primarily on weekly worship gatherings and the Passover–Shavuot festal cycle. No one had written down the exact day and year of Jesus' birth, though Luke's Gospel tells us that past-her-prime Elizabeth conceived a child with her husband Zechariah, followed six months later by the supernatural pregnancy of her virgin cousin Mary, "in the time of Herod king of Judea" (Luke 1:5).

Luke anchored the supernatural in place and time when he noted the census that drew Mary and her betrothed to Bethlehem in time for Jesus' birth (Luke 2:1-7). At the time, however, a teenage girl's pregnancy, attended by a blue-collar carpenter and a handful of shepherds in an overcrowded town, didn't make it onto any festal calendar.

As increasing numbers of Gentiles came into the church, leaders considered how to commemorate all of the movements of the life of Jesus. They recognized that, in an era where few could read the Scriptures for themselves, the calendar could be key to how disciples were made. December 25 was far from the only option used by the early church to mark the birth of Jesus. Many during that era marked a person's birthday by the day of his or her death. Calculations of Jesus' death date pointed to either March 25 or April 6,[1] and some suggested that on one of those two days, the angel Gabriel came to announce to Mary that she would bear a son (Luke 1:26-38). By counting forward nine months from those springtime dates, church leaders arrived at December 25 or January 6.

Some believers have insisted that the language used in John 1:14 was a clue pointing to a fall date for Jesus' birth, coinciding with the Feast of Tabernacles. By the fifth century AD, however, December 25 or January 6 won the debate. The Eastern (Orthodox) Church marked the birth of Jesus on January 6—also the date of Epiphany, which has a sacred story of its own (see chapter 13). The Roman Catholic Church, meanwhile, adopted December 25 as the birthday of Jesus. (The Protestant church would maintain this tradition.) Several more centuries would pass before "Christ's Mass," the Communion service celebrating his birth, would come into common usage. As the Christian calendar became more formalized, the Western Christmas feast day extended in length from one day to twelve days, through the Epiphany celebration on January 6.

From the beginning, Christmas was often an oil-and-vinegar blend of solemn celebration and pagan partying. Some have insisted that Christmas is nothing more than a spiritually sanitized version of a Roman pagan winter solstice festival known as the "Birthday of the Unconquered Sun." While this contention may have some merit, historian William Tighe makes this suggestion:

> *It is true that the first evidence of Christians celebrating December 25th as the date of the Lord's nativity comes from Rome . . . but there is evidence from both the Greek East and the Latin West that Christians attempted to figure out the date of Christ's birth long before they began to celebrate it liturgically, even in the second and third centuries. The evidence indicates, in fact, that the attribution of the date of December 25th was a by-product of attempts to determine when to celebrate his death and resurrection.* [2]

Both streams persisted in uneasy partnership for more than a thousand years, until the Protestant Reformation did some spiritual housecleaning. Seventeenth-century Reformers attempted to ban the holiday, citing both the lack of warrant for Christmas in

Scripture and the fleshly partying that marked the day.[3] Obviously, the ban didn't last.

KEEPING CHRISTMAS IN CHRIST

The partying of Christmas has spread to many cultures. The spiritual meaning of the day doesn't always spread with it. In Japan, Christmas is a day for fun and romance, almost like our modern American Valentine's Day. Christmas Eve celebrations in Ghana include drumming and dance; it is the beginning of the cocoa harvest in that African country, and Christmas celebrations are spread over a three-week period. Residents of Greenland mark the holiday by enjoying cakes and a whale blubber treat. "Little Jesus" brings gifts to Czech families while they're sharing their Christmas Eve dinner; he rings a bell when he leaves to let them know he's gone.[4]

Sorting fun family or cultural traditions from the celebration of the Incarnation can be a complicated exercise. A friend of mine was a pastor's daughter and came from a family with strong Swedish roots. Kathy cherished the rich holiday traditions, decorations, and foods her family had passed on from generation to generation. She couldn't imagine Christmas without baking hundreds of *pepparkakor* (spice cookies), loading a giant tree with heirloom ornaments, and spending lots of time with extended family. Kathy married a South American man from an extremely conservative church background. Since the holiday wasn't mentioned in the Bible, Gustavo's family eschewed any sort of Christmas celebration. He grew up without any connection to the holiday and found American Christmas an overwhelming extravaganza. Gustavo was perplexed by his wife's insistence that the way her family celebrated brought honor to Christ just as much as did his family's refusal to observe the holiday. The topic was one of the biggest issues in their newlywed life.

Each December brings us all a fresh wave of religious-themed Christmas controversy. Is it legal to display a Nativity scene on the grounds of the county courthouse? Should Christians boycott retailers whose clerks say "Happy Holidays" instead of "Merry Christmas"? What does it mean to keep Christ in Christmas?

The Christian calendar devotes twelve days to celebrating the miracle of the Incarnation. The feast days during that twelve-day period can help us step out of the commercial aspects of Christmas to consider how the Incarnation shapes us as a community of followers of Jesus:

> *December 26 (Feast of St. Stephen).* The day following Christmas is given to remember the generosity, courage, and faithfulness of Stephen, the New Testament's first martyr (Acts 6–7). Traditionally, this day has been a day dedicated to sharing the leftovers of Christmas feasts with the poor, in honor of Stephen's ministry as a deacon. It is also a day to focus on how we will respond to the incredible gift of Jesus with our lives. Stephen's life and death remind us that the babe in the manger is the beginning, not the end, of the Christmas story.

> *December 27 (Feast of St. John the Evangelist).* This feast day remembers John, who proclaimed the incarnation of Christ with both words and actions.

> *December 28 (Feast of the Holy Innocents).* This day is focused on remembering Herod's brutal massacre of all males ages two and under in Bethlehem in order to end Jesus' life (Matthew 2:16). Authors Edwin and Jennifer

Woodruff Tait offer a helpful orienting thought for us as we consider this day: "In celebrating the Holy Innocents, we remember the victims of abortion, of war, of abuse. We renew our faith that the coming of Christ brings hope to the most hopeless. And, in the most radical way possible, we confess that like the murdered children we are saved by the sheer mercy of Christ, not by our own doing or knowing."[5]

› *January 1 (Feast of the Circumcision of Christ).* Luke 2:21 tells us that on the eighth day after his birth, the Jewish Jesus was circumcised and named, following the commandments God gave to Abraham and Moses (Genesis 12:3; Leviticus 12:3). This day marked his full inclusion in the covenant community of the Chosen People.

It can be freeing to recognize that Christmas is a season, not a shopping deadline. The twelve days of Christmas invite us to receive afresh the gift of the Son in the same way his mother did: with our own "yes" of surrender to God (Luke 1:38). As Advent encourages us to prepare for Christmas by recognizing our need, the Christmas season is about welcoming Christ into every part of our lives.

EVERYDAY ETERNITY: CHRISTMAS

It's ironic that we often struggle to make space to be with God at Christmas. The Christmas season gives us an opportunity to contemplate what it means that God has come to dwell with us and how we can dwell daily in his presence. There are, however, some simple ways to enter into the twelve days of Christmas.

Focus on doing acts of simple generosity. Charitable giving

and acts of goodwill peak in the weeks leading up to Christmas. Offering a bit of your time in service to someone on the margins of your life during the postholiday letdown after December 25 reminds someone in need that God is with them, too. Scheduling a visit to a nursing home, babysitting for a frazzled young family, or calling on a neglected neighbor are simple ways to start.

If you attend a church that does not follow the Christian calendar, gathering for an unplugged contemplative service (for example, a service in the style of the Taizé religious community) can be a powerful post–December 25 tradition. These services typically include a simple opening song, a psalm, a read or sung response, a Scripture passage, silent meditation, intercession and prayer, and a closing song. The Taizé community (www.taize.fr) offers resources for planning such a gathering at your church.

To capture the true spirit of the Christian calendar's Christmas season, however, simply take some time to rest in the sheltering presence of God. You don't have to say or do anything. Receive his love. Welcome him afresh—or for the very first time—into your life.

13

THE LIGHT TO THE WORLD

Epiphany

I'VE ALWAYS LOVED those charming little manger scenes known as crèches. The rustic stable and beatific pastel characters seemed to me to be like a first-century version of a dollhouse. The most colorful characters in the group were always the three kings. They wore bright clothes and came with a bonus splash of golden paint on one of the gifts they carried—and maybe even on their exotic crowns or turbans.

I learned that St. Francis staged the first living Nativity display on Christmas Eve, 1223, in a cave near a town in Greccio, Italy. He was inspired to do so after he made a pilgrimage to Jesus' birthplace in the Holy Land.[1] The practice spread across Europe, and eventually someone got the clever idea to create figural representations of the living Nativities.

Many families display their entire manger scene when they decorate their homes for Christmas. The animals look so tranquil as they gather in rapt attention around the calm, always outward-reaching baby in the manger. It's the most religious of all Christmas decorations—a beacon among the tinsel, stockings, and plastic Santas, pointing us toward Bethlehem.

The completed crèche, however, isn't how Scripture presents Jesus' nativity. The shepherds may indeed have arrived on the scene within hours of Jesus' birth, but I doubt they brought a kneeling sheep along for their visit. The wise men may have arrived in Bethlehem as much as two years after Jesus' birth; Mary, Joseph, and Jesus were sheltered in a Bethlehem home when they came calling (Matthew 2:11).

The Christian calendar offers us a bit of clarity about the timing and meaning of these different visits. January 6, known as Epiphany ("manifestation," or "appearance"), is the day in which we join the Gentile wise men in their worship at Bethlehem. Epiphany brings the religious season of Christmas to a conclusion.

We may not know the precise number of wise men (or magi), but we do know the baby gifts they brought with them:

> › gold was a gift given by and to royalty;
> › myrrh was used as an embalming substance, painkiller, and sacred fragrance (Exodus 30:23; Psalm 45:8; Esther 2:12; Mark 15:23; John 19:19); and
> › incense was used in worship by many ancient cultures (Exodus 30:1; Leviticus 16:12-13).

These three gifts are symbols of the three roles used throughout the Old Testament to describe the coming Messiah: prophet, priest, and king.

Deuteronomy 18:15 (quoted in Acts 3:22-23) points toward a future anointed prophet. Jesus referred to himself as prophet (Luke 13:33; Matthew 13:57). He is also described as our High Priest

(Ephesians 5:2; 1 Timothy 2:5; 1 John 1:7; Hebrews 9:26-27; 10:12). And beyond his own frequent mentions about the Kingdom of God, Jesus is described as a king in Matthew 21:5 and 27:11. Revelation 19 portrays him as exercising royal authority, ruling over the people and dispensing judgment.

The magi's visit to the infant Jesus was a profound indicator that this child would fulfill the messianic promise to become the light to the nations (Isaiah 49:6). Author Robert Webber explains:

> *The Epiphany marks the turning point of the prophecy. The glory of God that has become incarnate is now manifested to the Magi, who represent the peoples of the world beyond Israel. From them the manifest glory of God will extend through the church to the whole world.*[2]

AHA! EPIPHANY!

The feast of Epiphany first appeared on the church calendar around the same time as Christmas. As the church split between West and East by the mid-eleventh century, the feast came to carry two different emphases.

In the East, the Orthodox family of churches gathered into one day the commemoration of Jesus' birth, childhood (circumcision, presentation/naming at the Temple), baptism by John, and the visit by the magi. Church leaders believed Epiphany, also known as Theophany ("manifestation of God to humanity"), was a fulfillment and celebration of the meaning of Chanukah, the Jewish Festival of Lights.[3]

In the West, the day had a single focus—the revelation of the Messiah to the Gentiles. The weeks following January 6 in the Western Christian calendar continue the themes introduced on

Epiphany. Congregations trace the life of Jesus through his baptism (Matthew 3:13-17; Mark 1:9-11; Luke 3:21-22; John 1:29-33) and first public miracle at the wedding at Cana (John 2:1-11). Other themes of the Epiphany season include Jesus' signs and wonders and the call to his disciples to follow him. The season of Epiphany concludes the Sunday before Lent, with the commemoration of Jesus' transfiguration (Matthew 17:1-13; Luke 9:28-36).

Epiphany (both the day and the season) reminds us of how Jesus filled full the mission God had given the Jewish people by seeking and saving those who'd been labeled "lost." He came to find those within his own Jewish community who recognized their distance from God. And he sought those outside this community, people to whom his own people had failed to reflect God's light. The wise men from the East present us with a powerful image of what it means to be a seeker, and Epiphany demonstrates the wonderful "aha!" of their discovery: The fulfillment of their seeking was an incarnate God who had come seeking them. Jesus' oft-quoted words capture the essence of this seek-and-save mission of love:

God so loved the world that he gave his one and only
Son, that whoever believes in him shall not perish but
have eternal life. For God did not send his Son into
the world to condemn the world, but to save the world
through him.   JOHN 3:16-17

Epiphany calls for a twofold response from each one of us. First, it is an invitation to worship as the wise men did. They demonstrated the essence of worship by giving up the comforts of home to follow the star and brought with them gifts befitting a ruler more powerful than they were. Second, Epiphany is an invitation to join Jesus in his mission. We live Epiphany as we show and tell the world that God is still seeking each one of us.

EVERYDAY ETERNITY: EPIPHANY

I think St. Francis was onto something when he created those living Nativity scenes in the thirteenth century. The life-size crèches served to underscore, in a way that a sermon or painting never could, that Jesus was born into our flesh-and-blood world. The earthy stink of animals crowded around a feeding trough, the sweat on the brows of those tasked with representing Joseph and Mary, and the piercing wail of a hungry baby all combine to demonstrate the stunning lengths to which God went in order to pursue each one of us. He who is fully God chose to become fully human in the most humble and helpless manner imaginable: a baby cradled in his mother's arms. The magi recognized Jesus' divinity in the midst of very unregal circumstances. Epiphany asks us if we will respond as the wise men did.

If you display a crèche in your home during this time of year, one simple way to connect with the journey of the wise men is to spread out the display. During Advent, set up the stable and animals. Then add Mary, Joseph, and the infant Jesus at Christmas. You can bring the shepherds and sheep in as well. On Epiphany, send the shepherds back to their day jobs in the Judean hills and bring the magi into the scene. Some families have the children move the wise men toward the manger each day until Epiphany.

The journey of the magi is only a part of the focus of Epiphany. Connecting with Jesus' mission to seek and save the lost is the larger theme of this season. Some liturgical churches observe the lovely custom of house blessings during this time of year. Because a home is meant to be a place of hospitality and welcome as well as a place from which its inhabitants are sent into the world, this practice is as relevant today as it was centuries ago. In the same way the manger was both a destination and a launchpad for Jesus, our homes serve both functions in our lives.

The core of this ritual includes a prayer of dedication over each room of the home and a chalked notation on an exterior door: "20 + C + M + B + 16." This means "In the year of our Lord 2016 [or whatever year it may be], Caspar, Melchior, Balthasar." These are the traditional names ascribed to the magi, but the letters C, M, and B also reference the Latin phrase *Christus mansionem benedicat*, which means "Christ bless this home."[4]

Whether you live in an urban condo, a suburban McMansion, or a yurt in the middle of the woods, this Epiphany ritual is a profound way to commit yourself, your space, and your moments and days to the mission of Jesus.

14

ASHES TO ASHES

Lent

LENT WAS A WORD once commonly used in the northern hemisphere to describe the lengthening days as winter moved toward spring.[1] Today, it tells a very specific story about the forty days leading up to Easter.

Forty is a significant number in the Bible. It usually symbolizes a period of trial, training, or testing:

> › God sent a flood to cleanse the earth, sparing Noah, his family, and the pairs of animals on the ark Noah built. It rained for forty days and forty nights (Genesis 7:12).
> › Moses lived forty years in Egypt, then forty years in Midian before God called him to lead his people from slavery to freedom (Acts 7:23; Exodus 7:7).
> › Moses spent forty nights on Mount Sinai when he received the Law (Exodus 24:18; 34:1-28).
> › Moses sent spies into the Promised Land for a forty-day reconnaissance mission (Numbers 13:25; 14:34).
> › The Chosen People spent forty years wandering in the

wilderness as God's judgment for their unbelief (Numbers 14:33; 32:13; Deuteronomy 2:7; 8:2; Joshua 5:6).

› When Israel disobeyed God, he gave them into the hands of their enemies for forty years (Judges 13:1).

› At Mount Horeb, Elijah fasted from food and water for forty days (1 Kings 19:8).

› The prophet Jonah spent forty days warning Nineveh that they would face destruction if they did not repent of their sins (Jonah 3:4).

› Ezekiel lay on his side for forty days as a prophetic portrait of Judah's sins (Ezekiel 4:6).

› After his baptism, Jesus spent forty days fasting in the wilderness before facing temptation from Satan (Matthew 4:1-11; Mark 4:12-13; Luke 4:1-13).

› Jesus appeared to many witnesses for forty days after his resurrection (Acts 1:3).

› Jesus' prophetic words about the destruction of the Temple (Matthew 24:1-2; Mark 13:1-2) came true in AD 70, within forty years (or one generation) of his crucifixion.[2]

The profound symbolism of the number forty wasn't wasted on leaders in the early church. A brief fast before the annual Pasch celebration (Easter Sunday; see chapter 16) expanded by the fourth century to become the forty-day period we now call Lent.

POST-EPIPHANY OR PRE-EASTER?

Some Christian calendar events like Easter and Pentecost have their origins in the Jewish feast cycle. Others have a fuzzier provenance. The origins of a forty-day Lent come from an interesting mix of sources. Pre-Pasch (Easter) fasting was common as a way in which Christians could prepare spiritually for this high point of the religious year. Since many baptisms were performed on Pasch, this preparation period eventually incorporated fasting and instruction for new converts. In this respect, Lent as we have it today is tied to Easter.

Believers in Egypt took a very literal approach to their Epiphany worship. After honoring Jesus' baptism in early January, they traced his footsteps into the next event in his ministry: his forty days of fasting before facing the Tempter in the desert. In this respect, then, Lent is tied to Epiphany.

In AD 325, Roman Emperor Constantine convened a council of church leaders with the goal of distilling the core beliefs and practices of the Christian faith. Among other things, they gathered the various opinions about Christian calendar events into a single authoritative declaration that would shape the worship year from that time.[3] Author Joan Chittister notes, "It is significant to realize that by the year 330, a Lenten season of forty days was common in the early church. That in itself, in a community that was only granted religious toleration in 313, is of no small significance."[4]

It took time for the church to sort out how to balance the forty-day period of abstinence and repentance represented in Lent with a weekly feast proclaiming the victory of Christ's resurrection on Sundays. Thus, as it is now practiced, Lent begins on Ash Wednesday and lasts forty-six calendar days: forty days plus six Sundays.

ASHES TO ASHES

The first year I attended a school where Gentiles were the overwhelming majority, I noticed a classmate with a strange smudge of black in the center of her forehead.

"Hey, you've got dirt on your face," I said. I thought I was doing her a favor when I reached up to wipe it away.

She recoiled in horror. "It's Ash Wednesday. That dirt is *supposed* to be there," she insisted.

I soon noticed many of my classmates were sporting dirty foreheads. I had no idea what this strange ritual was about, but as a self-conscious eighth grade girl, I was glad I didn't have to walk around like that all day.

I didn't know it then, but I learned (as we all do at some point in our lives) that mourning is a core reality of our earthly existence. We live in a world shaped by the effects of humanity's disconnection from God. That disconnection manifests itself in loss, sickness, and death. Whether it is a generalized awareness of our brokenness or a specific grief after the death of a loved one, Lent interrupts our regularly scheduled lives to reconnect us with the deepest need behind our pain: communion with God.

The act of kneeling to be marked by ashes, a practice that begins the season of Lent on what is known as Ash Wednesday, is a somber physical expression of humility. Ashes in Scripture are an outward sign of mourning or repentance (see, for example, Job 42:6; 2 Samuel 13:19; Esther 4:1, 3; Isaiah 61:3; Jeremiah 6:26; Ezekiel 27:30; Daniel 9:3; Matthew 11:21). The Anglican *Book of Common Prayer* includes an Ash Wednesday liturgy that offers participants a way to pray their desire for spiritual recalibration with both words and actions:

[The officiant reads the following words:] *Dear People of God: The first Christians observed with great devotion the days of our Lord's passion and resurrection, and it became the custom of the Church to prepare for them by a season of penitence and fasting. This season of Lent provided a time in which converts to the faith were prepared for Holy Baptism. It was also a time when those who, because of notorious sins, had been separated from the body of the faithful were reconciled by penitence and forgiveness, and restored to the fellowship of the Church. Thereby, the whole congregation was put in mind of the message of pardon and absolution set forth in the Gospel of our Savior, and of the need which all Christians continually have to renew their repentance and faith.*

I invite you, therefore, in the name of the Church, to the observance of a holy Lent, by self-examination and repentance; by prayer, fasting, and self-denial; and by reading and meditating on God's holy Word. And, to make a right beginning of repentance, and as a mark of our mortal nature, let us now kneel before the Lord, our maker and redeemer.

Silence is then kept for a time, all kneeling. If ashes are to be imposed, the officiant says the following prayer.

Almighty God, you have created us out of the dust of the earth: Grant that these ashes may be to us a sign of our mortality and penitence, that we may remember that it is only by your gracious gift that we are given everlasting life; through Jesus Christ our Savior. Amen.

The ashes are imposed with the following words.

Remember that you are dust, and to dust you shall return.[5]

Scripture readings for Ash Wednesday services include Joel 2:1-2, 12-17 (or Isaiah 58:1-12); Psalm 51 (or Psalm 103); 2 Corinthians 5:20–6:10; and Matthew 6:1-6, 16-21. Ash Wednesday sets the tone for the forty days of fasting that follow.

BLESSED ARE THE HUNGRY

Historically, the fasting practices associated with Lent have called for adherents to abstain from meat and all products coming from animals, including milk, eggs, and cheese. This kind of fast was reminiscent of Daniel's "vegetables only" fast (Daniel 10:2-3). Over time, strict fasting rules have been relaxed, though dietary restrictions are still a cornerstone of this season of the church year. Many streams following the church calendar ask members to participate in a full, no-food fast on Ash Wednesday and Good Friday. The (Eastern) Orthodox Church encourages members to abstain from food for the first three days of the Lenten cycle, then maintain a spare diet throughout the rest of Lent, with a few key feast day interruptions to the fast.[6]

Other traditions following the church calendar don't prescribe specific practices but instead encourage members to fast from something that's gotten a little too important to them during this season. This fast can include anything from restricting the use of social media to abstaining from sweet treats. Others have found it meaningful to include an Isaiah 58 focus on doing works of justice and mercy as part of their fast.

The disciples of John the Baptist asked Jesus why his disciples didn't fast in the same way that they and the Pharisees did. Jesus' answer to them defined the purpose and set the tone for Lenten fasting: "How can the guests of the bridegroom mourn while he is with them? The time will come when the bridegroom will be taken from them; then they will fast" (Matthew 9:15). Fasting puts us in touch with our deepest hungers and points us toward the only One who can satisfy them. Lenten fasts are meant to bring us face-to-face with our soul's emptiness. In a divine paradox, as we seek to be filled by him, we're freed to be used by him to pour out his love on his hungry, thirsty world. It's a profound way to walk with Jesus into the final week of Lent, known as Holy Week.

EVERYDAY ETERNITY: LENT

While fasting is an individual discipline possible at any point during the year, it takes on a communal nature during Lent. Many believers are participating in some form of fasting at the same time. This shared experience can strengthen each individual who elects to fast. Forty days can be a long time. When others around you are on the same spiritual trajectory you are, you may find encouragement to keep going—or, if you break your fast midstream, to begin again.

It's essential to remember fasting isn't a fast track to spiritual maturity. I've found fasting often exposes my areas of pride and self-sufficiency. It isn't until I've finished fasting that I discover how God was at work in me, confronting my little idols and recalibrating my unhealthy habits.

Here are a few suggestions if you're considering a fast for Lent this year:

> *Choose your fast with a specific spiritual goal in mind.* Rather than simply giving up, say, chocolate because you feel you should fast from something at Lent, it might be more helpful to think in terms of an area in your spiritual life that is not flourishing and focus your Lenten discipline on that area.

> *Journal your journey through Lent as a way of keeping yourself focused on what you're learning about God, yourself, and others.* Forty days is long enough to build a new habit. Journaling—or simply jotting a sentence or two about your fasting experience each day—can be a way of keeping yourself accountable to the discipline you've chosen. Journaling can also help you attend to the work the Holy Spirit is doing in and through your life.

> *Recognize that fasting can lead to a confrontation with the idols in your life.* When you abstain from something, you may discover that thing has a little more importance to you than you previously realized. If you'll pardon the pun, giving up chocolate for Lent won't earn you any spiritual brownie points. (Mostly because there's no such thing as "spiritual brownie points"!) However, it may present you with the realization that chocolate was a comfort for you in a way that only God is meant to be.

Lent is not a self-improvement program. Though the discipline of fasting may help us shed a few pounds or break a bad habit, this season of the Christian year isn't about us. The goal of Lent is to orient our souls toward Jerusalem, where we'll follow Jesus through the last week of his life. Lenten discipline prepares us to immerse ourselves into the life of Jesus during Holy Week.

15

WALKING TOWARD THE CROSS WITH JESUS

Holy Week

MAP IN HAND, my husband and I attempted to navigate the Via Dolorosa (Latin for "Way of Sorrows"). Pilgrims have been tracing Jesus' final steps through Jerusalem in a journey of devotion along the Via Dolorosa for nearly two thousand years. Some come with a Christian tour group. Some, like my husband and me, go it alone, using a map to navigate the bewildering warren of streets and sites within the meandering Church of the Holy Sepulchre, which houses the final five stops on this well-worn route.

Perhaps the most surprising thing for me about the Via Dolorosa journey was how short in distance it was. When I watched Hollywood movies about the crucifixion of Jesus, I imagined all the events leading him to Golgotha were miles apart. The Via Dolorosa is less than a half-mile in length.[1] Pilgrims take this quest amid swarms of locals selling souvenirs, carrying warm loaves of *simit* (sesame bread) on their heads, or yelling into cell phones over the din. It takes some effort and imagination to squeeze the sacred from the press of humanity in that place.

It is a temptation for many of us to read Scripture without ever fully participating in its story. Walking the Via Dolorosa was a vivid reminder for me that there are no bystanders in the crucifixion of Jesus. We each play a role: witness, critic, inquirer, executioner, beloved friend. Tracing Jesus' steps through the crowds toward the place of the skull, just as he had to do two thousand years ago, forced me to ask myself how I would have responded to him had I been standing on those packed streets. Would I be among the Passover-gathered crowds jeering him as he carried the cross on his bloodied back? Or would I be one of the few who wept as he passed me to the site of his execution?

The high point of the Christian year, Holy Week, is a ritualized journey through the final days of Jesus' life. During this week, we follow him from his "triumphal" arrival in Jerusalem to his execution by cross less than one week later. The rites of this week aren't glorified Bible study exercises. They help us uncover anew our present-moment part in God's salvation story.

HOLY WEEK ORIGINS

The very first followers of Jesus understood every Sunday as the day they'd gather to celebrate his resurrection. Still, there was an early impulse to add a yearly commemoration of this history-changing event. By the time Emperor Constantine made Christianity the official religion of the Roman Empire at the beginning of the fourth century, the basic structure of Holy Week was in place.

Holy Week is, technically, the final week of Lent, but the focus shifts during this week from the individual introspection to an active pursuit of Jesus through the last days of his earthly ministry. The three days before Easter (Maundy Thursday, Good Friday, and Holy Saturday) are stand-alone days in the Christian year focused on the final words and acts of Jesus, his suffering and passion, and his burial.

The Holy Week observance of Eastern (Orthodox) Christians usually occurs a week or two later than Western observance, but the nature of the week remains the same. (See appendix for date comparison.) The week ends at a boulder-covered grave. But it begins with a parade.

PALM SUNDAY

More than five hundred years before Jesus was born, the prophet Zechariah wrote,

> Rejoice greatly, Daughter Zion!
>> Shout, Daughter Jerusalem!
> See, your king comes to you,
>> righteous and victorious,
> lowly and riding on a donkey,
>> on a colt, the foal of a donkey.
>
> ZECHARIAH 9:9

In the ancient world, a king heading off to war would ride a swift, powerful horse (1 Kings 4:26; Isaiah 31:1-3). A king coming in peace would choose a humble, trusty donkey (2 Samuel 16:1-4). The people in Jerusalem expected their Savior to demonstrate his military superiority over the Romans. Jesus offered his response without saying a word.[2]

The crowds in and around the city became an impromptu welcoming committee for Jesus. His mode of transportation might not have been what they were expecting, but they were aching for someone—anyone—to set them free from Roman rule. They waved palm branches, an ancient symbol of victory, and chanted, "Hosanna!" (literally, "Save now!"). Perhaps they were hoping their welcome would convince Jesus to find himself a warhorse.

Lent helps us situate ourselves in this crowd. We have experienced the challenging combination of a long wait and slow change in our lives. We may be sure we'll recognize deliverance when we see it. Palm Sunday demonstrates how our expectations may blind us to what God is doing right before our eyes.

Palm Sunday services in many liturgical congregations are both celebratory and somber in nature. Congregants wave palm or other leafy branches and chant or sing their hosannas. Yet the traditional Scriptures to be read during the service include passages describing Jesus' obedience and humility (Philippians 2:6-9; Isaiah 50:4-7; Psalm 118:1-2, 19-29).

In most church traditions, the next few days of Holy Week are given to individual prayer and contemplation as we follow Jesus' movements around Jerusalem during the final days of his life. Some traditions (Catholic and Orthodox) place special emphasis on each day's worship service.

MONDAY: JESUS CLEANSES THE TEMPLE

Malachi 3:1-5 describes a "messenger of the covenant" who will come to purify and refine God's people so they will again worship him wholeheartedly. Matthew 21:12-27 and John 12:20-41 describe how Jesus disrupted both commerce and religious practice as he overturned merchants' tables in the Temple, then healed people who were blind and lame. The shouted "Hosannas!" of children who'd witnessed these things enraged religious leaders.

TUESDAY: JESUS WARNS HIS FRIENDS
AND SPEAKS TO HIS ENEMIES

On Tuesday of Holy Week, the Eastern (Orthodox) churches call on followers of Jesus to stay watchful and ready for the arrival of the Bridegroom. As an eleventh-hour warning to his disciples, Jesus told the parable of the ten virgins (Matthew 25:1-13). Five of these young women were prepared for their role in welcoming the groom, and five fell down on the job. The parable served as a prophetic portrait of his role as the Bridegroom coming to redeem his bride (Revelation 19:7; 21:2, 9; 22:17).

Jesus shared this story in the context of the events recorded in John 12:37-50. Here Jesus diagnosed the hard-hearted condition of those religious leaders who refused to recognize what God was doing in their midst through him. This act scandalized and radicalized Judas, who decided to turn Jesus over to the authorities.

WEDNESDAY: BETRAYAL OR WORSHIP?

In the Western church, Wednesday of Holy Week has been dubbed Spy Wednesday. The focus of the day is Judas' act of betrayal (Matthew 26:1-5, 14-16). In the Eastern (Orthodox) Church, however, this day is known as Holy and Great Wednesday. Worshippers are directed to the example of a woman who performed an extravagant act of worship by anointing Jesus at the home of a leper named Simon (Matthew 26:6-13). Betrayal or worship? Which choice will we make?

At this point of Holy Week, we follow Jesus up into the city for his final hours. He is about to simultaneously celebrate and become the Passover.

THE TRIDUUM

The final three days of Holy Week include Maundy Thursday, Good Friday, and Holy Saturday, or the Great Sabbath. Though these days are technically part of Lent, they have long been treated as a single, separate event in the Christian year. In the Western Church, this period is known as the *Triduum* ("TRI-doo-um," derived from the Latin for "three days").

The Triduum incorporated the way in which early believers readied themselves to celebrate the Resurrection each year. These spiritual preparations included the pre-Pasch fasts for and by new believers who would join the church in baptism. They also incorporated the church's custom of all-night vigils, or prayer watches, leading into a time of Resurrection Day rejoicing at daybreak.[3]

In the beginning, these practices grew organically out of the community's response to the work of the Holy Spirit among them. They became formal rituals as early believers expanded on them to encompass and memorialize the final movements of Jesus' life. Today, though each of the three days of the Triduum has a different emphasis, it is most helpful to understand them as a single movement in three parts.

Maundy Thursday. This day is given to remembering the events of the final night Jesus spent with his disciples (Matthew 25:17-35; Mark 14:12-26; Luke 22:7-38; John 13–17). Jesus gathered with his disciples for a Passover meal and adapted its elements in order to demonstrate for them what he'd come to do. He washed his disciples' feet, he infused cup and matzo with new meaning, and he gave those gathered with him a clear and specific commandment to love one another the way he loved them. In fact, the name Maundy Thursday comes from the Latin word *mandatum*, or "commandment."

While Maundy Thursday services in the Western church vary by tradition, they tend to be focused on foot washing and Communion. Some churches drape the cross in a shroud of fabric and strip any linens, Communion vessels, and decorative elements from the altar. This offers worshippers a vivid visual representation of what was set in motion when Christ was arrested at the end of this night with his disciples.

Some congregations expand Communion on Maundy Thursday to be a full Passover seder meal that highlights Jesus' words and actions. Others include a foot-washing ceremony, while still others include a Tenebrae service, either this night or as part of Good Friday services. *Tenebrae* (Latin for "shadows" or "darkness") is a somber service of Scripture and prayer: A series of lit candles are extinguished one by one throughout the service, slowly plunging the congregation into darkness.

When Eastern (Orthodox) Christians receive Communion during the day they call Holy Thursday, they pray this prayer:

Receive me Today, O Son of God, as a partaker of Thy Mystic Feast; for I will not speak of the Mystery to Thine enemies, I will not kiss Thee as did Judas, but as the thief I will confess Thee. Lord, remember me when I comest to Thy Kingdom.[4]

Good Friday. Author W. H. Auden once noted that while "Christmas and Easter can be subjects for poetry, . . . Good Friday, like Auschwitz, cannot."[5] Jesus, the One who was heralded as a hero days earlier, was rushed from one kangaroo court to the next before being sentenced to death by crucifixion on a killing ground outside the city known as Calvary, or Golgotha (Matthew 26:47-67; 27:11-26). The grieving of Lent moves us toward this most solemn day of the entire Christian year. It seems anything but good if viewed as a single, tragic event. But Good Friday is the day in which a good God worked out his divine plan of redemption for his broken, beloved creation.

While the first believers focused their gatherings on the events that happened three days later, by the fourth century AD, believers in Jerusalem had put feet to their pre-Easter fasting and prayer. Beginning on Maundy Thursday evening, believers began tracing the steps of their Savior from the Garden of Gethsemane through the sites of his trials. On Good Friday, they continued their solemn veneration, stopping to pray at each site named in the Gospels that made up Jesus' excruciating journey to Calvary.[6] At the site of his crucifixion, they'd read the Gospel eyewitness accounts until 3:00 p.m., the hour at which Jesus breathed his last. In the evening, believers would reconvene to remember his burial. Many would then stay in prayer through the night, contemplating the meaning of his death.[7]

These Jerusalem prayer pilgrimages along the Via Dolorosa birthed a devotional practice called the Stations of the Cross. By the fifth century, the practice had spread to other places, so those who couldn't make the pilgrimage to Jerusalem could trace Jesus' final hours in the churches where they worshipped.[8] Though the Stations of the Cross are no longer restricted to Good Friday observance alone, they originated there. The Stations of the Cross are often associated with the Catholic Church, but a number of Protestant traditions have developed their own version of this worship aid. Author Dennis Bratcher notes,

The Stations of the Cross is a liturgical way to reenact that journey as a meditation of worship, an act of devotion to God. To think that the event of Jesus' journey to the Cross was

a one time event in history is to misunderstand the role of remembering. For in remembering this event by walking the Stations of the Cross we are not just reenacting a 2,000 year old event. We are making our own journey, and in the process confessing our own dependence upon God.[9]

Other Christian traditions offer services that focus on the seven last sayings of Jesus on the cross. It is a day of deep mourning, though we do not grieve as those who live without hope. We know Resurrection Sunday follows Good Friday. But if we rush past this day without allowing ourselves to engage the meaning of Jesus' sacrifice for us, we risk diminishing its meaning and effect in our lives, our churches, and this world. If there is a day in our year to experience the greatness of the gulf between our time-bound humanity and the pure holiness of our eternal God, Good Friday is it. Standing at the edge of that gulf is where we can see the one on the cross most clearly. How will we respond to what we see? In scorn and derision, as so many in the crowd did? Or in stunned sorrow and recognition, as a handful of guards and committed followers did? Can we say with them, "Surely he was the Son of God" (Matthew 27:54)? Good Friday reminds us that there is no middle ground.

Holy Saturday, or the Great Sabbath. Jesus once told some Pharisees who asked to see a sign or miracle from him,

A wicked and adulterous generation asks for a sign! But none will be given it except the sign of the prophet Jonah. For as Jonah was three days and three nights in the belly of a huge fish, so the Son of Man will be three days and three nights in the heart of the earth.

MATTHEW 12:39-40

On Holy Saturday, we wait. We feel the weight of the events of Holy Week, and we realize that though it is Shabbat, we are not at peace. Not without Jesus.

In most liturgical traditions, Holy Saturday is the one day during the year in which Communion is not offered as part of a corporate worship service. In ancient times, an overnight vigil beginning on Saturday night would bring worshippers to the day that split history in two: the Resurrection. Today, sunrise services taking place on Easter morning are a nod to that vigil.

EVERYDAY ETERNITY: HOLY WEEK

Holy Week is rich with opportunities to participate in corporate worship, perhaps even in a church different from the one you usually attend. The week also lends itself to carving out personal time to contemplate the Cross. Of course, we could spend the rest of our days doing so and barely scratch the surface of what Jesus in his love did for us on Calvary. Attending a seder, participating in a foot-washing or Tenebrae service, or spending time the night before Easter at a vigil with brothers and sisters from a different Christian faith tradition can deepen your understanding of Holy Week and strengthen your connection with the larger body of Christ.

On an individual level, you may find that walking and praying through the Stations of the Cross is especially meaningful during Holy Week. Most Catholic churches and retreat centers have some form of the Stations as part of their architecture. If the church building is open and not being used for a service, you may be able to stop by and avail yourself of the Stations.

The classic Catholic Stations include a couple of stops on the journey to the cross that reflect traditional stories rather than solely the scriptural account. However, there are readily available alternate versions from both Catholic and Protestant sources that reflect only the details found in the Bible. The physical act of moving from station to station in reflection may not have the sights and sounds of the Via Dolorosa in Jerusalem, but it can lead you to the foot of the cross just the same.

16

LIVING IN RESURRECTION TIME

Easter

MY JEWISH PARENTS forbade me from attending a Christian church as long as I lived under their roof. My teenage mind reasoned that, if they were out of town for the weekend, we weren't technically living under the same roof. Therefore, on the Easter Sunday when they had left me home alone, I was free to attend a church service. I woke up at zero dark thirty so I could attend a 6:00 a.m. sunrise service with some of my friends from school.

I stepped into the darkness a few minutes before I needed to leave. The birds were calling to one another in the chill air. The sky was beginning to lighten; a deep gray-pink hue hugged the horizon. As I stood soaking in the moment, car keys in hand, the reality of what this morning meant in history welled up and flooded over me. I believed what I read in the Bible about Jesus, but in that predawn moment, time stood still and I tasted a moment of eternity.

Jesus had risen from the grave. He was alive!

It was as though I were there, peering over the shoulders of the women who came to his grave that Sunday morning after the long, hard, Great Sabbath of sorrow. My arms were full of the packages of burial spices I'd carried with me to Jesus' resting place so I could put my grief to some purpose and say good-bye in the company of friends who loved him as I did. I imagined we'd ask the soldiers stationed at the grave to help us roll the massive boulder away from the entrance in order to do the last thing we could for the one who had given everything for us.

I was there, tasting terror's bile in the confusion of prostrate soldiers and an empty grave. I could scarcely comprehend what a radiant being (an angel!) said with words that reported that history had been torn in two:

> Why do you look for the living among the dead? He is
> not here; he has risen! Remember how he told you, while
> he was still with you in Galilee: "The Son of Man must be
> delivered over to the hands of sinners, be crucified and on
> the third day be raised again."   LUKE 24:5-7

Jesus was alive! He had risen just as he said he would!

The transcendent moment faded gently back into time. I looked at my watch. It was 5:45 a.m. I couldn't wait to celebrate with those who were gathering at the church in the moments before dawn to sing his praises.

RESURRECTION DAY

Just before he entered Jerusalem on the back of a donkey, Jesus asked his friend Martha a prescient question: "I am the resurrection and the life. The one who believes in me will live, even though they die; and whoever lives by believing in me will never die. Do you believe this?" (John 11:25-26). The two of them were standing with a crowd of mourners at the sealed grave of Martha's recently deceased brother, Lazarus. She had no reason to hope. Yet her answer was one of complete trust and surrender: "'Yes, Lord,' she replied, 'I believe that you are the Messiah, the Son of God, who is to come into the world'" (John 11:27).

We've lived for two thousand years on the other side of Jesus' resurrection. The power of death has been broken for all eternity for all of God's beloved humanity. Yet some give in to the temptation to reduce belief to a matched set of neatly ordered intellectual facts. The word for believe (*pisteuo*) is used in this passage by both Jesus and Martha to express an entire commitment of one's whole self: heart, soul, mind, and strength.

The Resurrection requires this kind of belief from us. It gives us a restored relationship with the eternal, triune one. The Kingdom proclaimed by Jesus is expressed through the power of the Resurrection in us. We are not time-bound creatures but Resurrection sons and daughters.

RESURRECTION TIME

From the beginning, the Resurrection shaped the worship habits of the early church. Awe drove the first believers to celebrate the Resurrection together each Sunday, and it formed the early practice of a yearly Pasch.

As the observance of Pasch evolved and expanded over the first few centuries after the Resurrection to include the Triduum, the all-night prayer vigil that carried believers into the dawn of Resurrection Day came to include the kindling of a special Paschal candle. This candle represented the light of Christ as Sunday dawned.[1] In addition, a hymn of praise known as the Exsultet was chanted or sung to announce that Easter had arrived. Some of the words in this hymn can be traced back to the fourth century AD. It is a part of Easter morning celebration in both Orthodox and Catholic churches, as well as in many Protestant churches that use formal liturgy in their corporate worship.

Some of the ancient words in the Exsultet reference the way in which Jesus has become our Passover, and through his resurrection, the first fruits of Shavuot. Those feasts, as the words of the Exsultet proclaim, are the promise of salvation given and kept in the risen Son:

> *This is our Passover feast when Christ,*
> *the true Lamb, is slain,*
> *whose blood consecrates*
> *the homes of all believers.*
>
> *This is the night when you, Lord our God,*
> *first saved our ancestors in the faith;*
> *you delivered the people of Israel*
> *from their slavery*
> *and led them dry-shod through the sea. . . .*
>
> *Christ is risen, Christ and firstfruits*
> *of the holy harvest field,*
> *which will all its full abundance*
> *at his second coming yield.*
> *Then the golden ears of harvest*
> *will their heads before him wave,*
> *ripened by his glorious sunshine*
> *from the furrows of the grave.*[2]

EOSTRE, BUNNIES, AND BONNETS

I've known a few Christians who choose to avoid the contemporary celebrations of Easter and Christmas, citing the pagan roots of these festivals. A look back at early church history shows us that, while the church sifted through the issues surrounding the Pasch–Pentecost feast cycle during those first centuries, leaders were also trying to sort out what their relationship with their surrounding culture was to be. How were they to be "in the world, not of the world" (John 17:15-16; Romans 12:2)?

One pragmatic way in which the early church resolved this tension was to sync the festal calendar with the holidays and daily rhythms of the culture surrounding them. Roman society (as with most pagan cultures) had spring solstice fertility festivals, named in honor of various pagan goddesses, including the Teutonic goddess Eostre and the Assyrian Ishtar.[3] It's not hard to see the roots of the word *Easter* in the names of those goddesses. Author Bruce Chilton noted that the Gentile Christian community was willing to adapt the calendar of their own culture for purposes of worship:

> *Christians . . . adopted the solar cycle and intensified it, because they understood Christ as the true sun. In due course, the Julian calendar became the Church's, complete with the names of Roman months. When it became painfully obvious that the Julian calendar did not coincide with the cycles of the sun, Pope Gregory XIII gave his name to the calendrical reform in 1582 which shortened the year by ten days to accord with the solar cycle better. . . . Our "Good Friday" can take place on a day of the week named after a Norse fertility goddess . . . and no one seems much bothered.[4]*

Certainly secular culture today continues the association, with fertility symbols such as bunnies and eggs. But modern secular Easter celebrations also carry the remnants of specifically Christian tradition. New clothes, including those bonnets so popular a few generations ago, have their origins in the baptisms that took place on Easter morning. Converts wore white robes to the service, and eventually the practice spread so that everyone wore new clothes to church in celebration of new life.

Can chocolate bunnies share a day with paschal candles? The apostle Paul's counsel to the church in Rome about making space for individual conviction on foods and holiday observances (Romans 14:1-9) offers great wisdom in answering those questions. So do his words about not judging the practices of another, nor demanding that others adopt your convictions on a disputable matter (Romans 14:10-23).

I'll confess to enjoying a good chocolate bunny. I've been known to head to Walgreens the day after Easter to stock up on them when they're 60 percent off. I respect my brothers and sisters who eschew any semblance of pagan influence on their Resurrection celebrations. And I have plenty of grace for those who buy full-price chocolate bunnies and eat them for Easter breakfast in order to break a Lenten fast.

FIFTY DAYS OF EASTER

The tension over whether Easter is a pagan holiday or Christian one can be diffused by looking at how the Christian calendar describes it. Easter isn't a single day on the church calendar. Instead, it is a season that lasts fifty days until Pentecost, echoing the relationship on the Jewish calendar between Passover and Shavuot. While different church traditions take different approaches to this period, a basic outline for worship during this seven-week period usually focuses on living the reality of the Resurrection.

One helpful way I've learned to think about the Easter season (and the entire Christian year) has come as I've explored the *Revised Common Lectionary*. Used by many Protestant congregations who order their worship by the church year, it offers a carefully considered, time-tested structure to the public reading and preaching of Scripture. Each week's complementary Bible readings include an Old Testament passage, a psalm, a New Testament selection, and a segment of a Gospel. The seven Sundays from Resurrection Day to Pentecost are a part of each year's Easter season. A sampling of the suggested readings from the Gospels offers a look at the way in which the resurrection life of Jesus is proclaimed during this season:

> › Easter week 1: Celebration of the resurrection of Jesus (John 20:1-18)
> › Easter week 2: Jesus appears to Thomas (John 20:24-29)
> › Easter week 3: Jesus shares a meal with his disciples (Luke 24:36-48)
> › Easter week 4: The Good Shepherd lays down his life for his sheep (John 10:11-18)
> › Easter week 5: Abiding in the vine (John 15:1-8)
> › Easter week 6: Loving one another (John 15:9-17)
> › Easter week 7: Jesus' prayer for unity for us (John 17:6-19)[5]

Forty days after Easter (during Easter week 6), most congregations remember the ascension of Jesus (Luke 24:44-53). The celebration of Pentecost concludes the fifty-day Easter season.

EVERYDAY ETERNITY: RESURRECTION DAY

The New Testament writers placed a strong emphasis on the Resurrection. It was central to everything they said and did. Is its message and expression central in your life? At your church? Why or why not?

We have two thousand years of familiarity with the notion of living on the other side of the open tomb. We may gather in church services, saying words or singing songs about the Resurrection, yet fall prey to the subtle temptation to believe that merely reading, saying, or singing these words demonstrates our faith. The Resurrection invites a radical reordering of our hearts, souls, minds, and strength. Death is not the end of our "life sentence." Eternity is.

This reordering includes celebration—an overflow of wonder and pure, unfettered rejoicing in God's goodness. Our culture offers plenty of examples of celebrations, whether they're victory parades for a winning sports team or yearly New Year's Eve revelry. (It might even include a few chocolate bunnies!) In the church, we've sometimes missed the whole-life nature of Resurrection celebration. A church service alone does not suffice as our shared Easter rejoicing. Whether in the church or in our backyards, gatherings marked by hospitality, generosity, blessing, and Resurrection joy may have the flavor of a family reunion instead of a religious service.

And because Easter is both a season and our reality, we can extend our Resurrection celebrations far beyond a single Sunday. May our celebratory gatherings be an appetizer course for the banquet we'll one day share with the family of God (Revelation 19:9).

Some theologians have used the phrase "already but not yet" to describe what it is to live in the tension between the Resurrection and Christ's return to earth (Matthew 11:2-6; 25:31-46; 1 John 3:2; Revelation 1:7; 21:1-4). The apostle Paul wrote, "Now we see only a reflection as in a mirror; then we shall see face to face. Now I know in part; then I shall know fully, even as I am fully known" (1 Corinthians 13:12). He captured just what it is to live in the "already but not yet" in this life. Seeing face-to-face, knowing fully, and being known are our certain hopes because of the Resurrection. It is a hope we in the community of Christ are privileged to claim, share, and celebrate.

17

SIGNS, WONDERS, AND NEW COMMUNITY

Pentecost

IMAGINE YOU'RE A FIRST-CENTURY diaspora Jew. You're living in a small Jewish community located in Cyrene (modern-day Libya), in exile from your homeland. This year you're going to gather the family and make the nine-hundred-mile trek to Jerusalem to celebrate the feast of Shavuot. You may have wished every year you could participate in the pilgrim feast cycle with your people, but the distance made it an impossible dream. Until now.

This will probably be a once-in-a-lifetime trip for you and your kin. In Cyrene, you and your fellow Jews are a minority. Even so, you've fought assimilation, holding on to your spiritual identity in the fear of your one true God—even as you and your family have become woven into the fabric of everyday life in the city.

You arrive in holy Jerusalem and walk the streets on feast day, experiencing the joy of being among your people but also the disorientation of being so far away from all that is familiar. Suddenly, people are streaming away from the Temple and toward a house nearby. You're swept along with the throng. It is as though a volcano has erupted: A joyful cacophony of voices is crying out that the rogue teacher Jesus, executed at Passover time, has risen from the dead.

In the chaos, you realize you've understood the message of these joy-drunk disciples exactly, because you heard it in your mother tongue. Jesus' follower Peter quotes from the prophet Joel and the Psalms in a sermon that cuts through the chaos with clarity. His final words set your own heart on fire: "Let all Israel be assured of this: God has made this Jesus, whom you crucified, both Lord and Messiah" (Acts 2:36).

Unself-conscious, you raise your own ragged voice with thousands of others: "What must we do?"

To receive the forgiveness and cleansing from sin we need, Peter tells the crowd, we must repent and be baptized in the name of Jesus the Messiah. Then the Holy Spirit we'd experienced in wind, fire, and word will come upon us. "The promise is for you and your children and for all who are far off—for all whom the Lord our God will call" (Acts 2:39).

You and your family join three thousand other people responding to Peter's directive on that Shavuot.

For weeks afterward, you and your family elect to linger in Jerusalem. You don't have the funds to do so, but the generous sharing among this new community means you never know want. A sense of awe, thick and holy, fills your gatherings. You and your family find yourselves crammed in homes with other believers who have come from near and far—merchants and thieves and farmers and priests, clean and unclean—brought and held together in the power of the Holy Spirit (Acts 2:42-47).

THE PRESENCE OF GOD

The tongues of fire resting on the heads of Jesus' friends was an image familiar to the Jewish people. Though none who gathered for that first post-Resurrection Shavuot had ever seen a sign and wonder like it, they knew from Scripture it was a sign of God's imminent, glorious, holy presence. The word we often hear to describe this presence is *shekinah*, a form of the Hebrew word that means "he causes to dwell." Though the word itself is not found in Scripture, images of the *shekinah* are found throughout the Old Testament:

> › when God spoke to Moses out of the burning bush (Exodus 3);
> › when God led his people by a pillar of cloud by day and a pillar of fire by night (Exodus 13:20-22);
> › at the dedication of Solomon's Temple, when God's glory filled it so that the priests could not even perform their duties (2 Chronicles 5:14; 7:2);
> › in Ezekiel's prophetic vision of a coming judgment (Ezekiel 43:1-5); and
> › in Joel's prophetic promise of the Spirit being poured out on all of humankind in conjunction with the coming of the Messiah (Joel 2:28-29).

Jesus promised the Holy Spirit would be given to his followers (John 14:15-31; Acts 1:8). They didn't know when or how, but they obeyed his directive to wait in Jerusalem until the Holy Spirit came to baptize them with fire (Acts 1:4). The *shekinah* of God immersed them in the resurrection life of Jesus, filling them as he'd once filled the Temple and supernaturally empowering them to proclaim his glorious grace.

Paul uses the language of Shavuot, the feast whose focus was the offering of the first fruits of the new wheat crop, to speak about the resurrection of Jesus to his friends at Corinth:

> Christ has indeed been raised from the dead, the firstfruits of those who have fallen asleep. For since death came through a man, the resurrection of the dead comes also through a man. For as in Adam all die, so in Christ all will be made alive. But each in turn: Christ, the firstfruits; then, when he comes, those who belong to him. Then the end will come, when he hands over the kingdom to God the Father after he has destroyed all dominion, authority and power. For he must reign until he has put all his enemies under his feet. The last enemy to be destroyed is death.
>
> I CORINTHIANS 15:20-26

Some have dubbed the first Shavuot after the Resurrection as the birthday of the church. (For more about the feast of Shavuot, see chapter 5.) Shavuot's Greek name, *Pentecost*, is the marker in the Christian year that places believers again at the moment of explosive birth of this new community by the coming of the Holy Spirit (Acts 1:8). Author Joan Chittister wrote that Pentecost expresses the Resurrection:

> *Only here in this time, between the bursting open of the tomb and, fifty days later, the overflowing of the Holy Spirit, does the full awareness of what it is to live in Christ, with Christ, and through Christ finally dawn. Indeed, these first Christians were the first citizens of the new creation. Now began the breaking open of the future. Now the*

human community sees life lived as it is meant to be. Now creation is re-created.[1]

Within the limits of temporal time—within the "already but not yet"—this new creation is being birthed up to this present moment.

FIFTY DAYS

Pentecost had a place on the yearly Christian calendar from the second century. Pasch, the observance of the Resurrection, was the name for the entire fifty-day period between Easter Sunday and Pentecost Sunday. By the end of the third century, Pentecost was the name given to the final feast day of the fifty days. Over time, a liturgy and an eight-day vigil leading up to Pentecost formed around the day. These holy days were second only to Easter in importance for early believers.[2]

Because the date of Pentecost is calculated based on the date of Easter, which is derived from the lunar cycle, the earliest date in the Western church for Pentecost is May 10, and the latest date is June 13. In Western churches, Pentecost Sunday became an alternate day for baptisms for those who could not be baptized on Easter. The Eastern (Orthodox) church uses a different calculation for Easter and Pentecost.[3] (See the appendix for a comparison of dates.) The Western church then shifts from Pentecost to the Christian calendar season of Ordinary Time, until Advent ushers in a new Christian year. The Eastern church names the weeks until Advent "Sundays After Pentecost."

NOT JUST ME, BUT WE

Early believers recognized the outpouring of the Holy Spirit at Pentecost as a sign of the last days and the beginning of God's restoration of creation. When Peter referenced the apocalyptic words of the Old Testament prophet Joel on Shavuot, the predominately Jewish crowd understood he was telling them he believed they were at the dawn of the "eighth day" (Acts 2:14-41; Joel 2:28-32). The hope of a future new creation ushering in the reign of the Messiah was embedded in the structure of the three pilgrim feasts of Passover, Shavuot, and Sukkot.

The signs, wonders, and miracles were (and still are) road signs inviting Jew and Gentile alike—people from every tongue, tribe, and nation—into this new creation. The church is an "eighth day" community, existing to witness to the risen Jesus, empowered by the presence of the Holy Spirit in order to reconcile to the heavenly Father those who are far off and those who are near (Ephesians 2:17-18).

In our individualistic American culture, we often speak of the work of the Holy Spirit in personal terms: "*I* was convicted by the Holy Spirit"; "What is *my* spiritual gift?" While individuals respond or don't respond to the words and works of the Holy Spirit, Pentecost by definition was a shared, corporate event. Pastor and author Mark Roberts said,

> *In theory, the Spirit could have been poured out on the followers of Jesus when they were not gathered together. There are surely times when the Holy Spirit touches an individual who is alone in prayer, worship, or ministry to others. But the fact that the Spirit was given to a gathering of believers is not incidental. It underscores the centrality of the church in God's work in the world. The actions of the earliest Christians put all of this in boldface. The Holy Spirit is not only given to individuals, but also, in a sense to the gathered people of God.*[4]

One of the Scriptures read on Pentecost in churches using formal liturgy is the account of the building of the tower of Babel in Genesis 11:1-9. Rather than submitting to God's reign over them, the people had come together on the plain of Shinar to build a tower they felt would ensure they had power and control over their destiny. In response, God confused their tongues, scattering and dividing them from their building project and from one another.

God used the believers who spoke with other tongues on the day of Pentecost to overwrite Babel's legacy with a supernatural reversal. The eighth-day community birthed from Resurrection power demonstrated God's glory and proclaimed his reign over his world. The church's job description hasn't changed since that first Shavuot.

EVERYDAY ETERNITY: PENTECOST

Many of us who read and celebrate the Pentecost account struggle with what the church has become since that first glorious Shavuot after Jesus' resurrection. Whether we're reflecting on two thousand years of church history or considering the hurt caused by abuse of power by a church leader in a local congregation, we sorrow over the disconnect between Pentecost and our own experience.

That sorrow is a gift of God.

The eighth day is an "already and not yet" reality for us. We are landlocked in temporal time, complete with all the effects of present-tense brokenness, struggle, and sin. At the same time, we have access to the power of the Holy Spirit to teach, heal, comfort, challenge, and transform both us and those around us. Our sorrow in the present is a hardwired connection to the "*not yet,*" aiming us like a compass arrow toward our faithful, unchanging God.

As we celebrate what God has done for us by pouring out his

Holy Spirit, Pentecost can be a time to bring before God our sorrow and longing regarding any pain in our church experience. It can also serve as a time to receive from him all he wants to pour out on us as his people.

The book of Acts helps us see what we can expect. After the day of Pentecost, there was amazing numerical growth in the church. Acts records account after account of the supernatural love and courage of these early believers. It wasn't all a sparkly spiritual success story, however. There were lots of problems—false teachers, pretenders, rabble-rousers, and persecutors. Almost every New Testament letter was written to address problems in the church. These accounts give us an unvarnished picture of what it is to live in the space between the "already" and "not yet" of God's Kingdom.

Reflect on your own experience in the church. Where and when have you seen the Holy Spirit at work? In what ways have you seen human sinfulness veil God's glory? How have you reconciled the division between the two?

Perhaps Pentecost might launch a concerted season of prayer for either your local church or the global church. That prayer may be a step into healing from church-related past hurts and disappointments. I've learned that praying for the church, both local and global, connects me with God's heart for his body and reenergizes me for his extraordinary mission to the world.

18

RIGHT HERE, RIGHT NOW

Ordinary Time

BEIGE WALLS. Medium soft drinks. Elevator music. Basic cable. Plain white tees.

When we think about the meaning of the word *ordinary*, images like these may come to mind. To hear that the final season in the Christian year is called "Ordinary Time" is to imagine, perhaps, that there's nothing much happening during these weeks.

Ordinary comes from the Latin word *ordinarius*, which means "order." An ordinal number names a thing in its relationship to a set—for example, third in line. This is in contrast to cardinal numbers, which describe how many of a thing there are—for example, five crayons. The use of ordinal numbers in the context of the church year refers to the number of weeks between Pentecost and Advent, when a new year begins. The weeks are referred to by their ordinal numbers—in the Western church, starting with Trinity Sunday, the first Sunday after Pentecost and the first Sunday of Ordinary Time.[1]

Ordinary Time is not meant to be "ordinary time" for the people of God. This season is the way in which the Pentecost-empowered church focuses on spiritual growth through evangelism, service, and discipleship. Robert Webber summed up the rhythm of the Christian year like this:

> *Advent is a time to* wait.
> *Christmas is a time to* rejoice.
> *Epiphany is a time to* witness.
> *Lent is a time for* repentance and renewal.
> *The Great Triduum is a time to* enter death.
> *Easter is a time to* express the resurrected life.
> *After Pentecost is a time to* study and evangelize.
>
> *Of course we are to do all of these Christian practices all of the time. But a rule of thumb is that a specific time set aside for each facilitates and empowers our Christian experience at all times.*[2]

The Eastern (Orthodox) Church doesn't have a direct equivalent to Ordinary Time in its calendar.[3] Instead, the Eastern Church has a series of feasts commemorating other aspects of salvation history through the year.

MILE MARKERS ON THE JOURNEY THROUGH ORDINARY TIME

The spiritual focus of Ordinary Time emerged as the Western church continued to ponder the implications of the salvation story. The second half of the Christian year affords us an opportunity to follow Jesus into the world he loves and came to redeem.

During Ordinary Time, Catholic, Orthodox, and some Protestant traditions commemorate the lives of various saints—Christian heroes from all walks of life and every era of history. Depending on the church tradition, this season is punctuated with other days of note that mark the journey through this half of the Church year:

› *Trinity Sunday.* The first Sunday after Pentecost is given by churches in the West to focus on the revelation of the self-revealing God, who has made himself known to his creation as Father, Son, and Holy Spirit. Readings during liturgical worship services this day include Matthew 28:19; John 1:18; 15:26; and 2 Corinthians 13:14. Author Joan Chittister noted that Trinity Sunday is rooted in fourth- and fifth-century controversies about the nature of Jesus. "The answer to Arians, who claimed that Jesus was perfect human but not God, is a clear one: there are three persons or manifestations in this One God, and the Trinity is the relationship between them. The Trinity embraces both the divine as well as the human nature of Jesus. The feast was finally extended to the universal church in 1334."[4]

› *Reformation Day.* October 31 (or the Sunday nearest to it) is commemorated each year by Lutheran and some other Protestant congregations to honor the legacy of Martin Luther. This fiery sixteenth-century monk confronted the church leaders of his time about their unhealthy spiritual practices and beliefs. He was a key figure in what would come to be known as the Protestant Reformation.

› *All Saints Day.* While popular culture is focused on Halloween, with its roots in the ancient pagan Celtic festival of Samhain, many Western churches—most notably Catholic and Anglican congregations—mark November 1 with special worship services. The community of faith has long practiced a day of observance to honor the great cloud of faithful witnesses, saints, and martyrs who have gone before us (Hebrews 12:1). This day first found its way onto Christian calendars in response to the great number of Christians who died during the vicious years of persecution under Emperor Diocletian (AD 284–305). The Eastern (Orthodox) Church celebrates All Saints' Day the Sunday after Pentecost.

› *Christ the King Sunday.* The final Sunday of Ordinary Time is a recent addition to the Christian calendar. This Sunday is given to acknowledging the reign of the risen Lord Jesus over all (Isaiah 45:23; John 18:33; 36-37; Romans 14:11; Philippians 2:9-11; Revelation 1:8; 17:14). Roman Catholic Pope Pius XI instituted Christ the King Sunday in 1925 in order to counter the modern world's movement toward secularization. The day serves as a conclusion to Ordinary Time and a reminder that we are people looking ahead to the end of days—which we are again pointed to as the new church year begins the following week with Advent.

EVERYDAY ETERNITY: ORDINARY TIME

Ordinary Time occurs during the Northern Hemisphere's growing season, and one of the stories Jesus told gave me a vivid image of the spiritual focus of this period in the church year:

This is what the kingdom of God is like. A man scatters seed on the ground. Night and day, whether he sleeps or gets up, the seed sprouts and grows, though he does not know how. All by itself the soil produces grain—first the stalk, then the head, then the full kernel in the head. As

soon as the grain is ripe, he puts the sickle to it, because
the harvest has come.   MARK 4:26-29

As the resurrection life of Jesus takes root in day-by-day
discipleship in our lives, we will bear eternal fruit. This parable
emphasizes that we can't engineer, explain, or project-manage this
kind of growth. However, we are called to submit to the spiritual
growth and fruitfulness the Holy Spirit is cultivating in each one
of us and among all of us. Ordinary Time is a way in which we live
out the Pentecost reality: We are the church in the world and for
the world. In the Kingdom of God, nothing is ordinary.

One practice that can help you connect with the spiritual focus
of Ordinary Time is contemplation. Contemplation simply means
learning to be present to God in the everyday moments of your
life. Near the end of his life, seventeenth-century monk Brother
Lawrence wrote a series of letters describing how he learned to
commune with God during his years of nearly invisible service
to others as a cook. His gathered letters have become the beloved
devotional classic *The Practice of the Presence of God.*[5] His writing
has reminded generations of readers that the various spiritual disciplines that shaped his ordinary days were not the goal of his life.
Communion with God was.

> We must serve God in a holy freedom. We must work
> faithfully without trouble or disquiet, recalling our mind
> to God mildly and with tranquillity as often as we find it
> wandering from Him. It is, however, necessary to put our
> whole trust in God. We must lay aside all other cares and
> even some forms of devotion, though very good in themselves,
> yet such as one often engages in routinely. Those devotions are

only means to attain to the end. Once we have established a habit of the practice of the presence of God, we are then with Him who is our end.

We are well trained by our schedules and deadlines to look ahead in our lives. We are habituated by our regrets and sorrows to look back. Brother Lawrence learned the value of a contemplative life, which helped him learn to listen and respond in the moment to the promptings of the Holy Spirit in his life. Contemplation often leads to purposeful action.

Activism is the flip side of Ordinary Time spirituality. Intentionality about evangelism and service to others can take a countless variety of forms. This is not busywork or a way to get extra credit on your spiritual scorecard, however. A contemplative lifestyle will slow you down and teach you how to be more intentional in the way you use your time, talents, spiritual gifts, experience, or finances. God is at work in the world that he loves and wants to redeem. Activism flowing from contemplation positions you to join God where he is at work in this eternal place in temporal time.

CONCLUSION

It's About Time

A FEW YEARS AGO, child development researchers at Emory University asked a group of teens questions like "Do you know how your grandparents met?" and "Do you know some things that happened to your mom or dad when they were in school?"[1] The researchers found that adolescents who knew their family's history tended to have a stronger sense of emotional well-being and a greater confidence in their identity and their potential in life. The research team noted, "Family stories provide a sense of identity through time, and help children understand who they are in the world."[2]

The Jewish and the Christian calendars have been a kind of macro version of family stories. They have preserved the identities of adherents through history. Though the Jewish feasts were tied to a specific location, they were eventually "translated" into portable observances that have continued to define the Chosen People through two millennia of suffering and dispersion. The Christian calendar has provided the same overarching family story for believers, whether they've enjoyed the privilege of living in a majority Christian culture or been driven underground by persecution. In simplest terms, if every single spring I encounter in a Passover seder the reality that God is a deliverer, I can draw on that blessed reality when I'm facing a challenge on July 20, January 16, or fifteen minutes from now.

God has given us the privilege of discipling our children, grandchildren, and all who are following in our footsteps:

> Let each generation tell its children of your mighty acts;
> let them proclaim your power.
>
> PSALM 145:4, NLT

The calendar gives both form and substance to that privilege. As we celebrate God's mighty acts together, we are connecting the next generation with a past. That past includes our individual family stories but also enfolds them in a story much greater and more beautiful than our own. The feasts form the structure for the task of discipleship God has given us.

God tells us in Deuteronomy 6:7 we are to repeat and keep on repeating to our children the commands he has given us. This repetition was meant to take place within the structure of a family's daily life and inside the context of an entire community participating in a weekly and yearly rhythm of feasts, fasts, and festivals. The Jewish and Christian calendars I've described in this book remind us that we are part of a larger story. Both calendars frame time in terms of God's salvation story. These calendars do not exist so we can pencil in days of celebration and sorrow alongside dates in our oh-so-important schedules. Instead, these calendars demand we prioritize our time according to their rhythms, because their rhythms represent God's saving work in our lives and in the world.

A religious calendar certainly doesn't impart instant faithfulness to adherents. A cursory glance backward through history reminds us that the Chosen People had a calendar given to them by God, and they still drifted into idolatry. The church developed her own calendar and has her own messy, chaotic, divisive history. The Christian calendar reframed some of the Jewish feasts and flirted with blending some of the popular festivals of the majority pagan culture with their own worship. Were these latter impulses a poorly conceived attempt to make the church appear relevant to the culture? Or were they located in the desire to reclaim for God's glory these days that were once given to idol worship?

There's no single clear answer to those questions, other than to note that there truly is nothing new under the sun. The contemporary church continues to wrestle with the tension between Jesus' call to pursue holiness by being in the world but not of it (John 17:15-16) and his command to go into the world to share the gospel (Matthew 28:18-20).

In the case of both the Jewish and Christian calendars, our tension is resolved by living into the truth each in its own way proclaims to us: You and I are not the measure, or the focal point, of time. God is. Yet each calendar also tells us how valuable we are to him. He measures out of eternity each moment of our lives and gives us this time so we will learn his character and walk in his ways. We have been created to glorify God and to enjoy him forever.[3]

KEEPING TIME WITH GOD

When we submit our own urgent calendars to God's, we are acknowledging that we are not the boss of the universe, or even the generalissimo of our little corner of the world. We are also acknowledging that time has more than one dimension to it in a way our own calendars don't.

In Greek, there are two words for time: *chronos* and *kairos*. *Chronos* refers to sequential time: one o'clock, two o'clock, Wednesday, Thursday, Friday. For example, the creation narrative in Genesis 1:1–2:3 is a *chronos* account. When Herod asked the magi to tell him the precise time they saw the star announcing the birth of the Messiah (Matthew 2:7), he was asking a *chronos* question. You can see the root *chronos* in the word *chronological*. It is a *quantitative* way of describing time.

Kairos, on the other hand, is a *qualitative* way of expressing time. It describes an opportune moment or an appointed time for an action to take place. The word *kairos* is used eighty-one times in the New Testament.[4] When Jesus told his disciples to head to Jerusalem for the Feast of Tabernacles without him, it was an expression of *kairos* time: "*My time [kairos] is not yet here; for you any time will do*" (John 7:6, emphasis added). He used the word *kairos* to reference the end of days in the parable of the cruel tenants in Luke 20:9-19: "*At harvest time [kairos] he sent a servant to the tenants so they would give him some of the fruit of the vineyard. But the tenants beat him and sent him away empty-handed*" (verse 10, emphasis added). The Hebrew word *mo'ed*, used to describe the seven "appointed festivals" in Leviticus 23:2, carries the same connotation as *kairos*. (Other places where the word *mo'ed* is used include Genesis 17:21; Daniel 11:27, 35; and Habakkuk 2:3.)

Our sacred calendars convert *chronos* into *kairos*. These gatherings may take place according to a schedule on a temporal calendar, but they happen at the intersection of time and eternity.

In the New Testament book of Hebrews, Jesus is described in language that puts him infinitely above and beyond *chronos* time: "Jesus Christ is the same yesterday and today and forever"

(13:8). He experienced fully in the flesh what it was to live as part of the created order, existing within time and space. Yet simultaneously, because of his divine, eternal nature, his sacrifice is not limited to one particular place and moment: "We have been made holy through the sacrifice of the body of Jesus Christ once for all" (Hebrews 10:10). He is where time and eternity intersect. Our sacred calendars are reflections of his sacrifice.

NUMBERING OUR DAYS

When we pray, "Teach us to number our days, that we may gain a heart of wisdom" (Psalm 90:12), we are asking as *chronos*-bound creatures for God to give us *kairos*-shaped lives. The prayer underscores our status as pilgrims in time. Though both calendars I've described in this book cycle through each year, they are not merely orbiting the sun, going nowhere. Instead, each cyclical calendar is describing all of creation's journey toward its appointed time and destiny. These calendars are pointing us toward home.

In this respect, our sacred calendars are simply tools for discipleship. Each describes how we as individuals and as faith communities are to journey homeward. Each defines a "narrow path" through our days. In my own study and practice, I've discovered that each holy day or season offers a time to focus on one of the classic spiritual disciplines:

> › Sabbath invites us into a discipline of rest.
> › Passover invites us into a discipline of communion.
> › Shavuot invites us into a discipline of study.
> › Rosh Hashanah/Feast of Trumpets invites us into a discipline of repentance.
> › Yom Kippur invites us into a discipline of intercession.

> Sukkot/Feast of Tabernacles invites us into a discipline of hospitality.
> Advent invites us into a discipline of simplicity.
> Christmas invites us into a discipline of generosity.
> Epiphany invites us into a discipline of mission.
> Lent invites us into a discipline of fasting.
> Holy Week invites us into a discipline of contemplation.
> Easter invites us into a discipline of celebration.
> Pentecost invites us into a discipline of community.
> Ordinary Time invites us into a discipline of service.

BUT WHICH CALENDAR?

Perhaps you're waiting for me to announce the winner of a Jewish calendar versus Christian calendar throw down. Perhaps you're imagining I have one over the other to commend to you.

There is no throw down, nor a single "winner." I hope you've heard in my words how we lose eternal perspective when we allow the default setting of our own too-small, too-busy daily agendas to tell us the story we're living. That story tells us our sole value is in what we do—and its punch line is that nothing we can do will ever fill full our lives.

The Jewish calendar and the Christian calendar alike tell the story of a God who creates and redeems and is making all things new. There is no tidy way to sync or merge the two calendars at this point in *chronos* time, but I believe both calendars can play a role in our discipleship, in varying measures, for different groups.

Jesus' heart beat to the rhythm of the calendar of his people. This calendar had helped to define their identity since their deliverance from slavery in Egypt. After Jesus' resurrection and the destruction of the Temple a generation later, the young church's worship gradually transitioned from both the Jewish calendar and the worship practices of surrounding pagan cultures. Out of a combustible combination of Resurrection joy, anti-Jewish reaction by some influential early church leaders, and a multifront battle against various heresies infiltrating the Christian community, a new way to tell the story of Jesus evolved over *chronos* time. Sadly, in the process, the church as a whole often devalued her Jewish foundation.

STEWARDING TIME

I've heard dozens of sermons over the years about financial stewardship but precious few about how to steward time. Our sacred calendars provide us an opportunity to consider as individuals and as church communities how we're living eternity every day.

For individuals. It is important to remember that both the Jewish and the Christian calendars were intended for use by worshipping communities, not individuals. Even so, it is possible for an individual or family to use either the Jewish or Christian calendar (or some combination of both) as a devotional or discipleship tool in the home. Individuals or families may benefit from gathering a small group to learn—or better yet, to celebrate—together. You may have plenty of days where you're doing the equivalent of hustling to get three kids to three different places at the same time. But those days needn't define your experience of faith or growth in wisdom, if you purpose to live within redemption's yearly rhythms.

For congregations. If you're part of a church that relies on our civil calendar to mark time, this book may provoke conversation and prayerful reflection about the story your church is proclaiming to one another and the world around you. Certainly, sacred days and special seasons fall under the category of personal conviction and opinion, not dogma. However, in my experience most congregations who have never considered these questions tend to back-burner them out of habit, not deeply held conviction.

If you attend a church that's been using the church calendar, recognize the temptation toward rote worship. Over the years, I've heard many negative comments from friends worshipping in liturgical congregations; they've become wearied by the predictability of their congregation or denomination's worship rituals. Of course, there is temptation in every kind of congregation for worship to become routine. It is my prayer that you will recognize anew the story the Christian calendar is telling you about your Lord and that you'll value the soil from which this calendar has grown over time. It is your born-again birthright to explore the richness of your spiritual heritage. Form a class to study the feasts or the history of the Christian calendar; simply talking about these celebrations may enliven the celebrations themselves.

If you are part of the Jewish community, I hope you'll hear in my words high honor for the calendar I've known all my life—the one that includes the feasts and holy days on our calendar. This calendar has kept us as a community through dispersion and persecution and has shaped our understanding of God and the world in which we live in profound ways. I mark time by these days while recognizing that Jesus, my Jewish Messiah, fulfilled them. He did not in any way come to invalidate or delete our calendar any more than he came to put an end to our continued existence in the world.

I recognize that some from the Messianic community may not agree with my appreciation for both the Jewish feasts and the Christian calendar. There are those in this community who can't see any value or role for the church calendar, given those times in history when Christian feast days have become occasions to launch persecution of the Jewish community. I hope you'll hear in my words grace for all, along with a nudge to honor the faith expression of your Gentile brothers and sisters in Jesus, just as I am nudging them to do the very same thing for you.

Numbering our days via calendar is one way in which we learn and practice wisdom. The final day of *chronos* time is coming: We'll gather with the Lord for a never-ending family reunion. The community of faith will revel together in the grace and mercy of the Lamb of God. There will be no more tears, no more hunger, no more night, no more clocks. The numbering of days and pursuit of wisdom in this life will be translated for all who are his into the language of heaven's perfect joy. It will carry the sound of pilgrims coming home.

Then our only calendar will be eternity. Every day.

ACKNOWLEDGMENTS

One generation commends your works to another;
they tell of your mighty acts.

PSALM 145:4

This book exists because there were saints (and more than a few beloved scoundrels) throughout history who were faithful in recounting God's mighty acts from one generation to the next. I am looking forward to celebrating him with them for eternity.

I am grateful to the generations of my own family who've come after me: my children—Rachel, Ben and my daughter-in-law Sarah, and Jacob—and my grandsons, Gabriel and Lio. I'm thankful, too, for next-generation friends dear to my heart who've allowed me to commend God's works to them: Kale, Chrissy, and our godson, Charlie.

My husband, Bill, has been cheerleader, pray-er, fact checker, proofreader, and my best friend for thirty-six years and counting. This book grew out of our spiritual journey and our desire to tell others about the goodness of our Savior.

Bill and I have been a part of a number of different churches and Messianic congregations through the years. That breadth of experience gave me the spiritual vocabulary to tackle a project like this.

My critique crew waded through first drafts of most of these chapters and helped me make sense out of what I was trying to say. Carol Marshall, Kim Karpeles, Dr. Ingrid Faro, my husband, and my longtime prayer partner Meg Kausalik served the Lord and the readers of this book with their questions and insights.

The regular contributors to Christianity Today's Her.meneutics blog and my pals at Inkcreative.org have informed my writing life and enriched my faith with their intelligence, creativity, and courage. I'm grateful for the support and fellowship of the remarkable women of Digging Deeper, the Tuesday morning Bible study I've attended for the last three years. They've let me guinea-pig some of this material on them, and their questions nudged me forward on this project.

I had hoped I'd meet a few new thinking partners when I first enrolled in Northern Seminary in 2013. I did, and some of their work assisted me as I wrote this book.

Thanks go to Gabriele Udell for the initial push to tackle this project. I'm grateful for my agent, Dan Balow. His professionalism, humor, and encouragement have been a gift. And a giant *todah rabah* from the bottom of my heart to Dave Zimmerman and the team at NavPress. It is a joy and a privilege to work with you.

GLOSSARY

Challah (cHAH-luh)—A moist, egg-rich yeast bread. It's served in the form of a braided loaf at Shabbat. At Rosh Hashanah, the dough is coiled into a round form.

Diaspora (DEE-ah-spore-uh)—People dispersed from their homeland; often used to describe the state of the Jewish people not living in the land of Israel.

Gezerah (geh-zee-RAH)—A law or rule created by rabbis to keep people from violating one of God's laws; a "fence around the fence" of the Law.

Haggadah (hah-gah-DAH)—A word meaning "telling" used to describe the book containing the order of service for a Passover seder. There are also Haggadahs for some other holidays, but the Passover Haggadah is the most familiar one.

Havdalah (hahv-DA-luh)—Meaning "separation," the name of the short prayer ceremony that concludes the Sabbath.

Kvetch (kuh-VETCH)—A Yiddish word meaning to gripe or complain.

Lekayem (le-KAI-yem)—To uphold, establish, fulfill, complete, or accomplish.

Mishkan (mish-KAHN)—Tabernacle.

Mitzvah (MITZ-vah)—A good deed done out of religious duty.

Seder (SAY-dur)—Meaning "order," a seder is the formalized ritual meal Jewish families use to retell and experience anew the Exodus each year.

Sukkah (soo-KAH)—Booth, temporary dwelling. *Sukkot* is the plural form of the word.

Tchotchke (CHOCH-ka or CHOCH-key)—The Yiddish word for "trinket" or a dust-collecting bit of household bric-a-brac.

Torah (toe-RAH)—The Law given to Moses at Mount Sinai and contained in the first five books of the Old Testament.

SIDE-BY-SIDE
CALENDAR COMPARISON

THE FOLLOWING GRID gives you a picture of the way in which the Jewish feasts and the Christian calendars overlap and differ from each other. In addition to diverging from the Western (Catholic/Protestant) calendar, please note that the Eastern (Orthodox) Church uses three different calendars. This is because of the way in which the Western Gregorian calendar was adopted in various national churches in the East. The Orthodox dates on this calendar come from the Orthodox Church in America's website (http://oca.org/fs/paschal-cycle).

2017			
Month	**Jewish 5777-5778**	**Catholic/Protestant**	**Orthodox**
January		6th – Epiphany	7th – Christmas
February	10th – Tu B'Shvat		27th – Lent begins
March	11th – Purim	1st – Ash Wednesday	
April	10th – Passover 24th – Yom HaShoah	9th – Palm Sunday 13th – Holy Thursday 14th – Good Friday 16th – Easter	9th – Palm Sunday 16th – Easter
May	2nd – Israeli Independence Day 30th – Shavuot	25th – Ascension Day	25th – Feast of the Ascension
June		4th – Pentecost	4th – Pentecost
July	31st – Tisha B'Av		
August			
September	20th – Rosh Hashanah 5778 29th – Yom Kippur		
October	4th – Sukkot		
November			
December	12th – Chanukah	3rd – First Sunday of Advent 25th – Christmas	

RECIPES

WHAT WOULD A FEAST BE without food? Below, you'll find a few favorite holiday recipes you may wish to try when you gather around your table with family or friends on a feast day—or just an everyday Tuesday.

*   *   *   *

TIA SARAH'S SPECIAL HONEY CHALLAH
Sabbath

My grandsons speak both Spanish and English and call my daughter-in-law Tia (Aunt) Sarah. Tia Sarah is an excellent baker and has created her own delicious version of a traditional Sabbath egg bread recipe. To get an especially tender, flavorful challah, make sure to start your challah early in the day so you'll have time to allow your dough to rise three times.

- 2 teaspoons active dry yeast
- 2 teaspoons granulated sugar
- ½ cup plus 6 tablespoons warm water (approximately 100–110 degrees, comfortably warm when you place a few drops on the inside of your wrist, per the package directions on the yeast)
- ¼ cup vegetable oil plus extra oil to use for greasing the bowl in which the dough will rise

3 large eggs, at room temperature
2 teaspoons salt
3 teaspoons honey
¼ cup granulated sugar
4 cups flour (approximately—you may need up to 4½ cups,
    depending on the flour's moisture content and the humidity
    level of your kitchen)
2 tablespoons poppy seeds for sprinkling on top (optional)

In the bowl of a stand mixer,* dissolve the yeast and 2 teaspoons of granulated sugar in the warm water. Allow the yeast and sugar to dissolve for
a couple of minutes. The yeast-sugar mix should become bubbly, a sign
the yeast is growing.

Using a whisk attachment, blend the oil into the yeast. Next,
incorporate two of the eggs into the liquid, one at a time. Whisk in
the salt, honey, and ¼ cup of granulated sugar.

Switch to a dough hook and slowly begin to add in the flour. The
dough should be soft and slightly sticky. Continue mixing for 2 or 3
more minutes. Turn off the mixer and place the ball of dough onto a
lightly floured surface and knead with your hands until the dough ball
has a slightly blistered but smooth surface appearance. Knead by fold-
ing the ball of dough onto itself and pushing it down and away from
your body using the heels of your hands; then give the dough ball
a quarter-turn and repeat.

Clean and dry the mixing bowl you used to start your dough, then
grease it liberally with the vegetable oil. Place your kneaded ball of
dough into the bowl, turning it to coat its entire surface with oil. Cover
with plastic wrap or a hand towel and allow the dough to rise in a
warm, draft-free place for one hour. The dough should double in size.

Punch down the dough, re-cover it, and allow it to rise for another
hour in your refrigerator. This process slows the rising and infuses the
dough with flavor. After an hour, bring the dough out of the fridge
and allow it to return to room temperature. This should take an additional 30 minutes.

Divide the dough into four portions. Using your hands, roll each
portion into a long rope about 1½ to 2 inches in diameter. Pinch the
top of the four strands together, and begin to braid. You'll begin by

weaving the dough rope on your far left over, under, then over the other three strands. Continue the braid with the next rope now on your far left, again using the over, under, over pattern. Repeat until the entire loaf is braided. Tuck the ends of the braid underneath and place the dough on parchment paper on a large cookie sheet. Cover the challah with a towel and allow it to rise for an additional hour.

Preheat the oven to 375 degrees. Beat the remaining egg in a small bowl. Brush the egg wash gently across the surface of the challah. Sprinkle with poppy seeds if desired. Bake in the middle of the preheated oven for 30 to 40 minutes or until the loaf is golden brown. Cool the loaf on a rack before slicing.

Yield: 1 loaf (Double the recipe if you're planning to make the traditional two loaves for Shabbat.)

*If you don't have a stand mixer, you can use a hand mixer to blend your liquid ingredients and incorporate the first couple of cups of flour. After that, you can mix in the rest of the flour by hand. When you've incorporated about 3½ cups of the flour into the liquid, you can turn your dough onto a floured surface and work in the remaining flour by kneading it into the dough; then continue kneading the dough for an additional 5 to 10 minutes. It will take you about 10 to 15 minutes total to knead your dough by hand.

* * * *

CHRAIME (FISH SIMMERED IN SPICY TOMATO SAUCE)
Sabbath, Passover, Rosh Hashanah, Lent

This savory recipe comes from the North African Jewish community. Diaspora Jewish cooks learned to adapt local specialties so they'd fit within kosher cooking guidelines. Fish is a key component in many local Jewish cuisines, and this recipe has all the flavors of Middle Eastern cooking. Serve with plenty of warm bread or pita to mop up the savory sauce.

> 3 tablespoons extra-virgin olive oil
> 2 to 3 sweet red or green peppers, diced and seeds removed
> 1 Anaheim or poblano pepper, diced and seeds removed
> 5 to 6 garlic cloves, crushed
> 1 medium onion, chopped
> 1 tablespoon sweet Hungarian paprika
> 1½ teaspoons cumin
> Juice of one lemon
> Pinch of sugar
> 1 can (6 ounces) tomato paste
> 2 cups water
> 1½ pounds firm-fleshed white fish filets (tilapia, sea bass, snapper)
> ½ cup chopped cilantro leaves

Heat the oil in a large skillet. Add peppers, garlic, and onion, sautéing slowly until lightly browned (5 to 10 minutes). Add the paprika and cumin to the vegetables, stirring for 1 to 2 minutes more. Add the lemon juice, sugar, tomato paste, and water to the skillet. Stir together; then simmer the sauce on low heat for 10 to 15 minutes. Taste, adding salt and pepper as needed. Slip the fish into the sauce and simmer until the fish flakes easily with a fork. Sprinkle chopped cilantro over the top, salt and pepper to taste, and serve.

Yield: 3 to 4 servings

* * * *

DEBBIE'S BRISKET

Rosh Hashanah, Passover, Easter

I had a tried-and-true brisket recipe, but when I tasted my friend Debbie's version last Passover, I found a new favorite. If you're feeding a crowd, this slow-cooked brisket is a perfect do-ahead dish. The meat benefits from a day or two of resting time in your fridge before reheating to serve.

    2 large Spanish onions, sliced
    2 tablespoons paprika
    2 tablespoons garlic powder
    2 tablespoons dried chives
    1 tablespoon salt
    3 pounds first-cut beef brisket (not Irish corned beef brisket)
    ½ cup balsamic vinegar
    ⅓ cup honey

Preheat the oven to 400 degrees; then place the sliced onions in the bottom of a baking dish.

In a small bowl, mix the paprika, garlic powder, chives, and salt. Rub the mixture into the brisket, covering it thoroughly. Place the meat on top of the onions. Cover the dish tightly with foil and cook for one hour.

Meanwhile, combine the vinegar and honey in a small bowl. After the meat has cooked for an hour, remove from the oven, pour honey-vinegar mixture over the meat, and re-cover. Turn the oven down to 250 degrees and return the meat to the oven to cook for another 4 to 5 hours. Turn the meat every hour or so, which will allow it to absorb the juices. Remove from the oven and allow to cool fully before refrigerating, covered, for at least 24 hours.

Before serving, remove the meat from the juices and slice thinly against the grain. Return to the pan, cover, and heat in oven until warmed through.

Yield: 8 servings

*   *   *   *

ISRAELI SALAD
Any time

This simple chopped salad can be found on breakfast, lunch, and dinner tables across Israel. It is one of the standard accompaniments served with the country's ubiquitous and delicious falafel (fried chickpea ball) sandwiches.

  1 pound Persian cucumbers, diced, OR 1 pound regular cucumbers, peeled, seeded, and diced
  1 pound fresh ripe tomatoes, seeded and diced
  ⅓ cup finely minced onion OR one bunch scallions, sliced
  ½ cup minced fresh parsley
  3 tablespoons extra-virgin olive oil
  2 to 3 tablespoons fresh lemon juice

Combine all ingredients in a serving bowl. Allow the flavors to marry for a few minutes. Salt and pepper to taste. Serve at room temperature.

Yield: 3 to 4 servings

* * * *

PEARL'S NOODLE KUGEL

Rosh Hashana, Shavuot

There are a variety of kugel ("kuh-GUHL") recipes out there, but my heritage recipe for this noodle-cheese dish is sweet, rich, and simple. Serve squares of it warm as a side dish, or serve it at room temperature with fruit as a dessert. Or sneak a few bites from the pan of leftovers for breakfast the next morning.

    1 pound broad egg noodles
    3 tablespoons butter, cut into small pieces
    1 pound large curd cottage cheese
    1 pint sour cream
    3 eggs, beaten with fork
    2 tablespoons vanilla
    ½ cup granulated sugar
    Additional butter, sugar, and ground cinnamon and nutmeg for
        topping

Preheat the oven to 350 degrees. Parboil the noodles (cook about 75 percent of the cooking time suggested on the package), drain, and place in a large mixing bowl. Add butter to the bowl, mixing until melted. Gently fold in the cottage cheese and sour cream, then the eggs, vanilla, and sugar. Place the mixture in a well-buttered 9 × 13-inch casserole pan. Dot with additional butter, then sprinkle sugar, cinnamon, and nutmeg on top. Cover lightly with foil and bake for approximately 1 hour or until the center is set.

Yield: 12 servings

*   *   *   *

SYLVIA'S CHEESECAKE
Shavuot, Easter

This dense, not-too-sweet recipe has been in my family since the early 1970s. Sylvia was the Italian grandmother of a neighbor of ours. She made the best old-fashioned New York–style cheesecake, a classic treat among the Jewish community.

1½ cups graham cracker crumbs
4 tablespoons granulated sugar
½ teaspoon ground cinnamon
4 tablespoons melted butter

Combine the above ingredients in a medium bowl. Press into a buttered 9-inch springform pan to form the crust.

Juice of 1 lemon
24 ounces (3 packages) cream cheese, at room temperature
1 cup granulated sugar
5 eggs
1½ cups sour cream
2 tablespoons granulated sugar
1 teaspoon vanilla

Preheat the oven to 350 degrees. In a large mixing bowl, beat together the lemon juice, cream cheese, and 1 cup of sugar. Beat in the eggs one at a time until the mixture is light and fluffy. Pour over the crust. Bake for 45 minutes.

Remove from oven and let cool for approximately 20 minutes. Meanwhile, combine the sour cream, 2 tablespoons sugar, and vanilla in a small bowl. Spread over the slightly cooled cheesecake, then return to the oven for an additional 10 minutes.

Remove from the oven and let cool completely. Refrigerate overnight. The following day, remove the springform pan. Serve as is or with fresh berries.

Yield: 12 servings

*   *   *   *

GINGER-MOLASSES CRINKLES
Christmas

I first began making these spicy old-fashioned cookies three decades ago. Nothing fills the house with the scent of Christmas more than these chewy gems. These versatile cookies are just as delicious in the middle of the summer served alongside a tall glass of lemonade.

¾ cup vegetable shortening
½ cup white sugar, plus approximately ¼ cup extra to roll the cookies after mixing the dough
½ cup brown sugar
¼ cup molasses
1 egg
2½ cups flour
1½ teaspoons baking soda
1 teaspoon ground ginger
1 teaspoon ground cinnamon
½ teaspoon ground cardamom
½ teaspoon ground nutmeg
Pinch (⅛ teaspoon or less) of salt

Preheat oven to 350 degrees. Beat the shortening and sugars together until blended; then blend in the molasses and egg. Next, mix in all the dry ingredients until thoroughly combined.

Place the ¼ cup of white sugar into a shallow dish. Form the dough into balls approximately one inch in diameter; then roll the top half of each ball into the sugar. Place on cookie sheets, unsugared-side down. Bake for approximately 6 to 8 minutes or until barely browned. Let cool on cookie sheets for 1 to 2 minutes before removing to racks to finish cooling.

Yield: approximately 4 dozen

* * * *

ADDITIONAL RESOURCES

THIS LIST OF ONLINE RESOURCES is offered as a starting point for you to further explore these subjects. Inclusion on the list does not indicate the author's or publisher's unqualified endorsement of all content on these websites.

JEWISH FEASTS
Messianic Jewish Publishers and Resources (messianicjewish.net): This one-stop shop offers a wide variety of books, including Messianic Jewish Passover haggadahs, gifts, and more.

Israel 365 (israel365.com/store/): This Israel-based online store offers a variety of Judaica (Jewish ceremonial art and objects).

Judaism.com (judaism.com): Another online source for Judaica, books by Jewish authors, and more.

JEWISH EVANGELISM
Chosen People Ministries (www.chosenpeople.com): This organization has been focused on Jewish evangelism since 1894.

Jewish Voice Ministries (www.jewishvoice.org): This media-based ministry is involved in evangelism and a variety of mercy ministries.

Jews for Jesus (www.jewsforjesus.org): Probably the most well known of the groups involved in Jewish evangelism, their website offers a host of resources about how to share the Good News with your Jewish friends. Lots of cultural and holiday resources too.

Lausanne Consultation on Jewish Evangelism (lcje.net): The Lausanne Movement, which encourages networking, learning, and prayer around issues related to missions, is the umbrella group under which those committed to Jewish missions gather.

MESSIANIC JEWISH DISCIPLESHIP

Caspari Center (www.caspari.com): My husband and I have been involved with Caspari for the last several years. This Jerusalem-based ministry provides teacher training, leadership training, workshops, and much more to Messianic congregations throughout Israel. It is involved in reconciliation and educational ministry both in Israel and beyond.

Hebrew for Christians (www.hebrew4christians.com): This website is packed with biblical Hebrew language study resources as well as information about holidays, Jewish life cycle events, and the relationship between Judaism and Christianity.

First Fruits of Zion (www.ffoz.org): Articles and study materials about the Jewish foundations of the Christian faith.

THE CHRISTIAN YEAR

Creative Communications for the Parish (www.creativecommunications.com): Church supplies, devotional materials, and materials for every season of the church year.

Christian Resource Institute (www.crivoice.org): This broadly ecumenical website offers a wealth of resources about worship, the Lectionary, the Christian year, theology, and more.

Liturgy Training Publications (www.ltp.org): This Catholic online store offers a host of church year resources.

Salt of the Earth (www.thechristiancalendar.com/sample.htm): This creative approach to a calendar synthesizes the Gregorian calendar and the church calendar.

CHRISTIAN YEAR PRAYER AND DISCIPLESHIP

Book of Common Prayer (www.bcponline.com): The prayer book of the Anglican Communion offers liturgy for every season of the church year, Lectionary readings, catechism (instruction), and more.

Fellowship of St. James Daily Devotional Guide (www.fsj.org/new/devotional-guide .php): A church year daily reading guide that synthesizes readings from the Orthodox, Catholic, Lutheran, and Anglican traditions.

Northumbria Community (www.northumbriacommunity.org/offices/how-to-use -daily-office/): The life of this Protestant community in England is based on the ancient discipline of fixed-hour prayer through the Christian year.

Revised Common Lectionary (www.lectionary.library.vanderbilt.edu/): This site houses a clear, easy-to-follow version of the *Revised Common Lectionary*, which is used by many mainline Protestant Churches.

NOTES

INTRODUCTION: TAKE MY MOMENTS AND MY DAYS

1. Quoted in Paul Steinberg, *Celebrating the Jewish Year: The Fall Holidays* (Philadelphia: Jewish Publication Society, 2007), 54.

CHAPTER 1: MEASURING TIME, BEING MEASURED BY TIME

1. Thomas Cahill, *The Gifts of the Jews: How a Tribe of Desert Nomads Changed the Way Everyone Thinks and Feels* (New York: Doubleday, 1998), 94.
2. Tracey R. Rich, "Jewish Calendar," Judaism 101, accessed September 22, 2015, http://www.jewfaq.org/calendar.htm.

CHAPTER 2: IN THE BEGINNING

1. Tom Olson, "Need Wisdom? Number Your Days," June 12, 2014, accessed September 29, 2015, http://www.unlockingthebible.org/need-wisdom-number -days/.
2. Quoted by Harold S. Kushner in Hayyim Schauss, *The Jewish Festivals: A Guide to Their History and Observance* (New York: Knopf Doubleday, 1996), ix.
3. Abraham Joshua Heschel, *The Sabbath: Its Meaning for Modern Man* (New York: Farrar, Straus and Giroux, 1979), 7–8.
4. Heschel, *The Sabbath*, 96.
5. "Vital Statistics: Jewish Population in the United States, by State," Jewish Virtual Library, accessed September 29, 2015, http://www.jewishvirtuallibrary.org/jsource /US-Israel/usjewpop.html.
6. "Movements of Judaism," Judaism 101, accessed September 29, 2015, http://www .jewfaq.org/movement.htm.
7. "A Portrait of Jewish Americans," Pew Research Center, October 1, 2013, accessed September 29, 2015, http://www.pewforum.org/2013/10/01/jewish-american -beliefs-attitudes-culture-survey/.
8. On the number of Messianic Jews in the United States, see "The Land Belongs to Israel!" Messianic Jewish Alliance of America, July 6, 2007, accessed September 29,

2015, http://www.mjaa.org/site/News2?page=NewsArticle&id=5142&security=1& news_iv_ctrl=1022. On where Messianic Jews worship, see "Jewish Roots," Chosen People Ministries, accessed September 29, 2015, http://www.chosenpeople.com/main /jewish-roots/304-messianic-congregations-and-the-modern-messianic-movement.

CHAPTER 3: DAY OF YES, DAY OF REST

1. Abraham Joshua Heschel, *The Sabbath: Its Meaning for Modern Man* (New York: Farrar, Straus and Giroux, 1979), 10.
2. "The Fourth Commandment," Hebrew for Christians, accessed September 29, 2015, http://www.hebrew4christians.com/Scripture/Torah/Ten_Cmds/Fourth _Cmd/fourth_cmd.html.
3. Cornelius Plantinga, *Not the Way It's Supposed to Be: A Breviary of Sin* (Grand Rapids: Eerdmans, 1995), 10.
4. Rich Robinson, *Christ in the Sabbath* (Chicago: Moody, 2014), 159.
5. Lauren F. Winner, *Mudhouse Sabbath: An Invitation to a Life of Spiritual Discipline* (Brewster, MA: Paraclete, 2007), 9, 10.

CHAPTER 4: INTO FREEDOM

1. Anne Cohen, "101 Years of the Maxwell House Haggadah," Forward, March 23, 2013, accessed November 23, 2015, http://blogs.forward.com/the-arty-semite /173621/-years-of-the-maxwell-house-haggadah/.
2. Lois Tverberg, "What Does It Mean to 'Fulfill the Law'?" En-Gedi Resource Center, accessed November 23, 2015, http://www.egrc.net/articles/director /articles_director_1006.html.
3. Tverberg, "What Does It Mean to 'Fulfill the Law'?"
4. Rabbi Ismar Schorsch, "Easter and Passover," My Jewish Learning, accessed November 23, 2015, http://www.myjewishlearning.com/article/easter-and-passover/2/.

CHAPTER 5: FIFTY DAYS AND FIRST FRUITS

1. "American Bible Society's State of the Bible 2015," American Bible Society, accessed May 19, 2016, http://www.americanbible.org/uploads/content/State _of_the_Bible_2015_report.pdf.

CHAPTER 6: MAY YOU BE INSCRIBED IN THE BOOK OF LIFE

1. Paul Steinberg, *Celebrating the Jewish Year: The Fall Holidays* (Philadelphia: Jewish Publication Society, 2007), 51.
2. See Matthew 24:3, 27, 37, 39; 1 Corinthians 15:23; 1 Thessalonians 2:19; 3:13; 4:15; 5:23; 2 Thessalonians 2:1, 8-9; Hebrews 10:24; James 5:7-8; 2 Peter 1:16; 3:4, 12; and 1 John 2:28.

CHAPTER 7: ATONEMENT AND MERCY

1. Sydney Taylor, *More All-of-a-Kind Family* (New York: Random House Children's Books, 1954), Kindle locations 329–38.
2. Leviticus 16 details the specific instructions God gave for this annual Day of Atonement.

3. 1 Peter 1:18-19; 1 John 1:7; Revelation 1:5.
4. Alfred Edersheim, *The Life and Times of Jesus the Messiah,* vol. 2 (London: Longmans, Green and Co., 1883), 609.
5. Daniel Stökl Ben Ezra, *The Impact of Yom Kippur on Early Christianity: The Day of Atonement from the Second Temple to the Fifth Century,* Wissenschaftliche Untersuchungen zum Neuen Testament 163 (Tübingen: Mohr Siebeck, 2003), 331.

CHAPTER 8: GOD WITH US, US WITH GOD
1. Michael Strassfeld, *The Jewish Holidays* (New York: Harper Collins, 1985), 144.
2. Paul Steinberg, *Celebrating the Jewish Year: The Fall Holidays* (Philadelphia: Jewish Publication Society, 2007), 124.
3. *Mishneh Torah* (Laws of the Festivals) 6:18, quoted in Yanki Tauber, "The Ushpizin," Chabad, accessed November 25, 2015, http://www.chabad.org/holidays/Jewish NewYear/template_cdo/aid/571505/jewish/The-Ushpizin.htm.

CHAPTER 9: STONES OF REMEMBRANCE
1. Tracey R. Rich, "Tu B'Shevat," Judaism 101, accessed November 25, 2015, http://www.jewfaq.org/holiday8.htm.
2. "Forestry and Green Innovations," Jewish National Fund, accessed November 25, 2015, http://www.jnf.org/work-we-do/our-projects/forestry-ecology/?_ga=1 .244565573.1567322057.1422820294.
3. Elie Wiesel, preface to the new translation of *Night* (New York: Hill and Wang, 2006), xv.
4. Rabbi Mordechai Becher, "History of Events on Tisha B'Av," Ohr Somayach, accessed November 25, 2015, http://ohr.edu/1088.

CHAPTER 10: FROM HERE TO THERE
1. Andrew Louth, ed., *Early Christian Writings: The Apostolic Fathers* (New York: Penguin, 1987), 73.
2. Didache 14:1, from "The Didache or Teachings of the Apostles," Early Christian Writings, accessed November 25, 2015, http://www.earlychristianwritings.com/text /didache-lightfoot.html.
3. "Against the Jews" teaching was an entire body of work in the early and medieval church designed to demonstrate the superiority of the gospel over the Chosen People. The seeds of this teaching burst into bloom when Constantine made Christianity the official religion of the Roman Empire in AD 313. The once-persecuted Christians became the persecutors of the Jews, believing they were serving God by doing so.
4. At Constantine's request, this council hammered out what has come to be known as the Nicene Creed, which established boundary markers that defined mainstream Christian faith.
5. If the full moon occurred on a Sunday, church leaders determined that Easter would be delayed a week so it wouldn't share a date with the Jewish Passover. Elisheva Carlebach, *Palaces of Time: Jewish Calendar and Culture in Early Modern Europe* (London: Belknap Press, 2011), 117.

6. Oskar Skarsaune, *In the Shadow of the Temple: Jewish Influences on Early Christianity* (Downers Grove, IL: IVP, 2002), 432.

7. Unless otherwise noted, this section will highlight the cycle used by the Western Church. The Orthodox Church calendar varies slightly from these dates, which come from the Roman Catholic calendar. Among the various national/ethnic Orthodox churches, there are some slight variations from country to country, based on the solar calendar each has elected to use. For instance, the Russian and Polish Orthodox churches follow the Julian calendar; the Greek, Romanian, and Orthodox Church in American churches follow the Revised Julian calendar. Lutherans and Anglicans are usually in sync with the Roman Catholic calendar. Churches that were birthed out of the Calvinist and Anabaptist Reformation (such as Presbyterians and Brethren, respectively) do not use the church calendar to shape their worship cycle. "Church Calendar," *Orthodox Wiki*, accessed November 25, 2015, http://orthodoxwiki.org/Church_Calendar. See appendix for a comparison of the dating of the Jewish feasts and the key Christian calendars.

8. Laurence Hull Stookey, *Calendar: Christ's Time for the Church* (Nashville: Abingdon Press, 1996), 22.

CHAPTER 11: LONGING FOR HOME

1. Everett Ferguson, *Baptism in the Early Church: History, Theology, and Liturgy in the First Five Centuries* (Grand Rapids: Eerdmans, 2009), 239.

2. Patricia B. Buckland, *Advent to Pentecost: A History of the Christian Year* (Wilton, CT: Morehouse-Barlow Co., 1979), 27.

3. Marcellino D'Ambrosio, "Christmas Countdown: The O Antiphons," CatholicMom .com, December 7, 2014, accessed May 19, 2016, http://catholicmom.com/2014/12 /17/christmas-countdown-the-o-antiphons/.

4. William Saunders, "The History of the Advent Wreath," Catholic Education Resource Center, accessed December 8, 2015, http://www.catholiceducation.org /en/culture/catholic-contributions/the-history-of-the-advent-wreath.html.

5. "History of a Festival of Nine Lessons and Carols," King's College Cambridge, accessed December 8, 2015, http://www.kings.cam.ac.uk/events/chapel-services /nine-lessons/history.html.

6. Sarah Pulliam Bailey, "12 Advent Calendars That Are Just As Commercialized as Christmas," Religion News Service, November 28, 2014, accessed December 8, 2015, http://www.religionnews.com/2014/11/28/12-of-the-internets-most -beautiful-bizarre-advent-calendars/.

7. Robert E. Webber, *Ancient-Future Time: Forming Spirituality through the Christian Year* (Grand Rapids: Baker, 2004), 52.

CHAPTER 12: WELCOMING THE WORD MADE FLESH

1. Thomas J. Talley, *The Origins of the Liturgical Year* (New York: Pueblo Press, 1986), 91.

2. William J. Tighe, "Calculating Christmas," *Touchstone Journal*, December 2003,

accessed December 9, 2015, http://www.touchstonemag.com/archives/article
.php?id=16-10-012-v.

3. Patricia B. Buckland, *Advent to Pentecost: A History of the Christian Year* (Wilton, CT: Morehouse-Barlow Co., 1979), 36–37.

4. "Christmas around the World," whychristmas?com, accessed December 9, 2015, http://www.whychristmas.com/cultures/.

5. Edwin and Jennifer Woodruff Tait, "The Real Twelve Days of Christmas," *Christianity Today*, August 8, 2008, accessed December 9, 2015, http://www .christianitytoday.com/ch/news/2004/dec24.html?start=1.

CHAPTER 13: THE LIGHT TO THE WORLD

1. Kathleen Manning, "Who Invented the Nativity Scene?" *U.S. Catholic*, December 2012, accessed December 9, 2015, http://www.uscatholic.org/church/2012 /10/who-invented-nativity-scene.

2. Robert E. Webber, *Ancient-Future Time: Forming Spirituality through the Christian Year* (Grand Rapids: Baker, 2004), Kindle locations 1244–49.

3. "The Church Year: Epiphany," accessed December 9, 2015, http://oca.org /orthodoxy/the-orthodox-faith/worship/the-church-year/epiphany.

4. "Epiphany (Theophany)," ChurchYear.Net, accessed December 9, 2015, http:// www.churchyear.net/epiphany.html.

CHAPTER 14: ASHES TO ASHES

1. "Lent," Online Etymology Dictionary, accessed December 9, 2015, http:// www.etymonline.com/index.php?term=Lent.

2. "The Meaning of Numbers: The Number 40," BibleStudy.org, accessed December 15, 2015, http://www.biblestudy.org/bibleref/meaning-of-numbers-in-bible/40 .html; and Jack Wellman, "What Does the Number Forty (40) Mean or Represent in the Bible?" *Christian Crier* (blog), October 3, 2014, accessed December 15, 2015, at http://www.patheos.com/blogs/christiancrier/2014/10/03/what-does-the -number-forty-40-mean-or-represent-in-the-bible/.

3. Nicholas V. Russo, "The Early History of Lent," Baylor University, accessed December 9, 2015, http://www.baylor.edu/content/services/document.ph /193181.pdf.

4. Joan Chittister, *The Liturgical Year: The Spiraling Adventure of the Spiritual Life* (Nashville: Nelson, 2009), 108.

5. "Ash Wednesday," *The (Online) Book of Common Prayer*, accessed December 9, 2015, http://www.bcponline.org/SpecialDays/ashwed.html.

6. "Fasting and Great Lent," The Self-ruled Antiochian Orthodox Christian Archdiocese of North America, accessed December 9, 2015, at http://www.antiochian.org/fasting -great-lent.

CHAPTER 15: WALKING TOWARD THE CROSS WITH JESUS

1. Wendy Bumgardner, "Walking the Via Dolorosa," verywell, April 3, 2015, accessed December 9, 2015, http://walking.about.com/od/traileurope/ig/Via-Dolorosa/. See also "Via Dolorosa, Jerusalem," Sacred Destinations, accessed December 9, 2015, http://www.sacred-destinations.com/israel/jerusalem-via-dolorosa.

2. Andreas J. Köstenberger, *Exegetical Commentary on the New Testament: John* (Grand Rapids: Baker, 2004), 371.

3. "The Paschal Triduum (Easter Triduum)," ChurchYear.Net, accessed December 9, 2015, http://www.churchyear.net/triduum.html.

4. Rev. George Mastrantonis, "Holy Week in the Eastern Orthodox Church," Greek Orthodox Archdiocese of America, accessed December 9, 2015, http://www.goarch .org/ourfaith/ourfaith8432.

5. W. H. Auden, *A Certain World* (New York: Viking, 1970), n.p.

6. Arrest of Jesus: Mark 14:46; Jesus tried by the Sanhedrin: Matthew 26:57-67; Jesus tried by Pilate: John 18:28-40; Jesus flogged, crown of thorns forced on his head: John 19:1; Jesus carries his cross: John 19:17; Simon of Cyrene is forced to help Jesus carry his cross: Mark 15:21; Jesus speaks to the women grieving for him: Luke 23:27-31; Jesus nailed to the cross: John 19:18; two thieves speak to him: Matthew 27:38-44; Jesus cares for his mother: John 19:25-27; Jesus dies on the cross: John 19:28-37; Jesus is laid in a tomb: John 19:38-42.

7. Robert E. Webber, *Ancient-Future Time: Forming Spirituality through the Christian Year* (Grand Rapids: Baker, 2004), Kindle locations 2250–52.

8. Fr. William Saunders, "How Did the Stations of the Cross Begin?" Catholic Education Resource Center, accessed December 9, 2015, http://www.catholic education.org/en/culture/catholic-contributions/how-did-the-stations-of-the-cross -begin.html.

9. Dennis Bratcher, "The Cross as a Journey," The Voice, accessed December 9, 2015, http://www.crivoice.org/stations.html. This site contains an excellent introduction to the Stations of the Cross, plus a helpful liturgy for Protestant use.

CHAPTER 16: LIVING IN RESURRECTION TIME

1. Dom Jerome Gassner, "The Exsultet," CatholicCulture.org, accessed December 10, 2015, http://www.catholicculture.org/culture/library/view.cfm?recnum=6341.

2. "Prayers on a Theme of Easter," Faith and Worship, accessed December 10, 2015, http://www.faithandworship.com/prayers_Easter.htm#ixzz3WFVUqub1.

3. "Where Did 'Easter' Get Its Name?" ChristianAnswers.Net, accessed December 15, 2015, http://www.christiananswers.net/q-eden/edn-t020.html; Heather McDougall, "The Pagan Roots of Easter," theguardian, April 3, 2010, accessed December 15, 2015, http://www.theguardian.com/commentisfree/belief/2010 /apr/03/easter-pagan-symbolism; "Easter: Its Pagan Origins," ReligiousTolerance .org, accessed December 15, 2015, http://www.religioustolerance.org/easter1.htm.

4. Bruce Chilton, *Redeeming Time: The Wisdom of Ancient Jewish and Christian Festal Calendars* (Grand Rapids: Baker Academic, 2002), 100.

5. *Revised Common Lectionary*, Vanderbilt Divinity Library, accessed December 10, 2015, http://lectionary.library.vanderbilt.edu/texts.php?id=93.

CHAPTER 17: SIGNS, WONDERS, AND NEW COMMUNITY

1. Joan Chittister, *The Liturgical Year: The Spiraling Adventure of the Spiritual Life* (Nashville: Nelson, 2009), 171–73.
2. William J. Collinge, *Historical Dictionary of Catholicism* (Lanham, UK: Scarecrow Press/Rowman & Littlefield, 2012), 340.
3. "What Is Pentecost Sunday (Whitsunday)?" ChurchYear.Net, accessed December 10, 2015, http://www.churchyear.net/pentecost.html.
4. Mark D. Roberts, "What Is Pentecost and Why Does It Matter?" *Reflections on Christ, Church, and Culture* (blog), accessed December 10, 2015, http://www.patheos.com/blogs/markdroberts/series/what-is-pentecost-why-does-it-matter/#ixzz3WZnCPY5K.

CHAPTER 18: RIGHT HERE, RIGHT NOW

1. Some traditions also refer to the weeks between Epiphany and Lent as Ordinary Time. For the purposes of this chapter, I'll only be focusing on the weeks following Pentecost, comprising the second half of the Christian year.
2. Robert E. Webber, *Ancient-Future Time: Forming Spirituality through the Christian Year* (Grand Rapids: Baker, 2004), Kindle locations 3156–62.
3. "The Liturgical Year," The Nazarean Way, accessed December 15, 2015, http://www.thenazareneway.com/liturgical_year.htm.
4. Joan Chittister, *The Liturgical Year: The Spiraling Adventure of the Spiritual Life* (Nashville: Nelson, 2009), 186–87.
5. An online version of the text of this book is available at http://thepracticeofthe presenceofgod.com/onlinetext/.

CONCLUSION: IT'S ABOUT TIME

1. Marshall P. Duke, "What Are the Stories That Bind Us?" *Huffington Post*, March 23, 2013, accessed December 15, 2015, http://www.huffingtonpost.com/marshall-p-duke/the-stories-that-bind-us-_b_2918975.html.
2. "Children Benefit if They Know about Their Relatives, Study Finds," Emory University, March 3, 2010, accessed December 15, 2015, http://shared.web.emory.edu/emory/news/releases/2010/03/children-benefit-if-they-know-about-their-relatives-study-finds.html#.VTe_na3BzGc.
3. Westminster Shorter Cathechism, question #1, accessed May 19, 2016, http://www.opc.org/sc.html.
4. "Kairos," Bible Study Tools, accessed December 15, 2015, http://www.biblestudytools.com/lexicons/greek/nas/kairos.html.

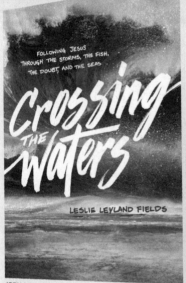

Glen Eyrie

CASTLE AND CONFERENCE CENTER

Glen Eyrie is a place where, for a few sacred moments, guests can set aside their troubles and catch their breath. Nestled on 800 breathtaking acres with 97 lodging rooms, The Glen is the perfect setting for hosting conferences, retreats, special events, and corporate or ministry meetings.

Spiritual Retreats • Conferences • Day Events • Private Teas
Castle Tours • Family Reunions • Social Events • Overnight Stays

GLEN EYRIE

3820 N. 30th St
Colorado Springs, CO 80904
719-634-0808
gleneyrie.org

CP1168